All writings were
compiled from past
blog posts from
JoeCoffeyTalk.com

A Cup of Inspiration
by Joe Coffey

Table of Contents

PART I
Family is in the Church

Family is in the Church

God designed the Church as a body of believers, a family to work together in His name. Just as a family is called to sacrifice, protect, and strengthen one another, the Church has been created to accept all comers, to offer support, encouragement, and to build up one another in the pursuit of becoming one with God.

Remember:

Husbands, love your wives, just as Christ loved the church and gave himself up for her to make her holy, cleansing her by the washing with water through the word, and to present her to himself as a radiant church, without stain or wrinkle or any other blemish, but holy and blameless.

- Ephesians 5:25-27

The following stories range from the joys of parenthood to the camaraderie found through persevering what some would declare as insurmountable obstacles (and for some those are one in the same). These are accounts focused on teamwork, encouragement and finding that the Church is your family and you are a child of God Himself.

Adoption

Imagine you come home from work and there is a kid working in your yard. He's mowing the grass and picking up the clippings and you think to yourself, "Ok, that's unusual but kind of cool." And you let him keep doing it. Every day for a month he's out there doing something in your yard. He is edging the flowerbeds and weeding and your lawn looks better than it has in years.

After a month all of a sudden you hear the door open and he comes in with two suitcases, goes upstairs, puts them in a bedroom and comes back down. He takes a seat at the kitchen table and you look at him with your mouth open. You finally say, "Ummmm...what's up?" He says, "Well, I've been working outside for a month in your yard and I just thought it was time to make this my family. Mom, Dad, I'm home."

Thinking he could become part of the family on his own merit by working in the yard and then saying in effect, "You owe me" is ludicrous. Adoption must be the choice of the parents. Adoption is grace by its very nature.

People wonder why they can't work their way to heaven. It is because it is family. No one works their way into a family. For me to bundle up all of my good works and walk into heaven announcing I am home is crazy. If I am going to be adopted it is by the will of the Father. Adoption is grace and it is wonderful.

Here is the thing, if you find yourself at the table of the King, you have been adopted. You are chosen and there is nothing more wonderful in all the world.

Verse for Reflection:

For it is by grace you have been saved, through faith—and it is not of yourselves, it is the gift of God—not by works, so that no one can boast.

- Ephesians 2:8-9

Like It Was Yesterday

I just got home from visiting my daughter and new grandson. I sat and held the little guy as he slept all curled up on my chest. It seems like just yesterday I fell asleep with his mother curled up in the same way and about the same size. But it was not yesterday. It was 24 years ago.

There is a certain poignancy with becoming a grandfather. Watching my children leave home has been my least favorite part of getting old. I don't mind getting up to go to the bathroom at night or forgetting where I left my keys or the gray hair that keeps popping up. But does age have to take away my children? And yet today I sat with my grandson and looked at my daughter sitting on the couch across from me and I felt a joy that wrapped itself around the sadness. My daughter glows with the beauty of a new mother. She has all the markings of being a great mom. She has had a great one to watch and learn from so it really should not be a surprise. I guess it still is though. I walk into her spotless apartment and think of how her room at home always looked like a clothes bomb had just gone off. I watch how she handles her baby and changes his diaper and wonder why it was so hard to get her to put away her dishes. And yet, here she is being a mom and she is already so good at it.

Growing old is no picnic. I know I sound as if I am 100. I don't mean to but I do know that an empty nest puts me past the halfway point of this race. Anyway, growing old may not be a picnic but there are certain benefits. My daughter had to grow up and I had to give her away before she could give to me the joy that was mine today.

I think of a sermon I have given. God gave His son away those many years ago. If God was to have the joy of holding you and me to His chest then there was no other way. So He gave and because He gave I get to lay my head on His chest and sleep as soundly as little Liam did today with me.

Verse for Reflection:

I pray that you ... may have power, together with all the saints, to grasp how wide and long and high and deep is the love of Christ.

- Ephesians 3:17-19

Pg. 4

Good Friday

I received the text at 1:57 a.m. "He's here" is all it said. It was all I needed to know.

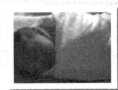

The text was from my son-in-law. He was letting me know my grandson Connor Joseph had broken out into this world. It was 1:57 a.m. on April 19th. It was also my 52nd birthday. It was also my dad's 78th birthday. It also marked the 110th year since my grandfather's birth.

As you can see, Connor Joseph arrived right on time—ten days before the due date and by natural delivery. How wild is that! We are way too much into timing here at the Coffey household.

My daughter sent a photo of newly born Connor and as my wife and I sat looking at it we felt our hearts being stolen. It's what children do. You have a child and the moment they come out they grab your heart and say, "This is mine from this day forward till the day I die." It is violent. It is wonderful. It is terrifying.

The movie "Love Story" had a famous and pretty ridiculous line where a character says, "Love is never having to say you're sorry." I don't know if I have ever heard anything that makes less sense. Love is something very much different. Love is giving your heart away to such an extent that you become completely vulnerable. When a child is born no one knows what kind of joy or heartache that child will bring. All we know is that those of us who love the child are in for the ride no matter where it takes us.

Today is Good Friday. It is the day when we remember where God Himself took the ride. Scripture tells us "God so loved the world" and that sounds warm and nice. But love is never just warm and nice . . . at least not real love. Real love takes enormous time and energy. Real love hurts. Real love bleeds.

And so it is, that on this Friday, we remember that when God so loved the world He bled out on a cross. It was not just warm and nice. It was a love that was violent and brutal and stronger than death. That is what makes this Friday so good.

The author of the Song of Songs writes of this love at the end of the book when he says,

Pg. 5

Love is as strong as death, as unyielding as the grave. It burns like a blazing fire. Many waters cannot quench love and rivers cannot wash it away. If a man were to give all the possessions of his house in exchange for this love it would be utterly scorned.

Such is the love of God for you and He proved it on a Friday many years ago. Worship Him and know that no child on earth has been loved more powerfully than you.

Verse for Reflection:

A Psalm for giving thanks. Make a joyful noise to the Lord, all the earth! Serve the Lord with gladness! Come into his presence with singing! Know that the Lord, he is God! It is he who made us, and we are his; we are his people, and the sheep of his pasture. Enter his gates with thanksgiving, and his courts with praise! Give thanks to him; bless his name! For the Lord is good; his steadfast love endures forever, and his faithfulness to all generations.

- Psalm 100:1-5

The Talk

Saturday was Homecoming at my daughter's school. It was her junior year so it was crucial that she get asked. She did and so all is well. Saturday came and it was time for me to have my talk with her date. I talk to all the guys who want to go out with my daughters. I would love to do it while cleaning my guns but I don't own any.

Anyway, I took him down to the basement and we talked. My daughters always want to know what I say. I don't tell them but I think they already know. I already knew this kid and I liked him. I like all of my daughter's friends which is a really good place to be. So, I started just by letting him know how important Becca is to me. I talk to him about the umbrella of protection that a father puts around his family. I feel like it is my responsibility to protect Becca physically, emotionally, and spiritually.

I tell him that tonight, just tonight, that is his responsibility. That means that if she is cold you give her your coat, if she is lonely you give her company, if she is scared you give her your arm, if she is tired you bring her home. I told him I hold him responsible for anything and everything that happens to my daughter that night. She is like a Porsche. You bring her home dinged and I will ding you. It is a good talk and one I like giving. I like it because it reminds me of what it means to be a dad and how great it is to have a daughter I would give my life for. It also, like everything else, reminds me of Jesus and His Father. How much must God the Father love us that He gave His Son in the greatest exchange of all?!

So, I watch my daughter leave smiling and I watch the boy open the door for her and I pray and then I thank my Father in heaven for grace greater than all my sin.

Verse for Reflection:

Jesus answered, 'I am the way, the truth, and the life. No one comes to the Father, but through me.'

- John 14:6

Pg. 7

Bending the Map

A friend who knows I love adventure sent me a book for Christmas. The title of the book is "Deep Survival" and it is a study on why certain people survive calamities and others perish. It is fascinating. I just read a section on what happens when people get lost in the wilderness. Getting lost while I am driving can be frustrating but getting lost in the wild can often be fatal. The author does a great job of communicating the absolute terror that accompanies lostness. This is how he describes it:

"Psychologists have observed that one of the most basic human needs, beginning at birth, is to be gazed upon by another. Mothers throughout the world have been observed spending long periods staring into the eyes of their babies with a characteristic tilt of the head. To be seen is to be real, and without another to gaze upon us, we are nothing. Part of the terror of being lost stems from the idea of never being seen again."

The fear is so great that people who feel like they may be lost begin to do what experts call "bending the map." The hiker has a map but the map no longer matches up with the environment they find themselves in. They are lost. But instead of admitting that to themselves they begin to question the map. They are trying to make the world conform to them instead of them conforming to the world. I found that whole section fascinating.

I sit with people all the time who are starting to move away from God in one way or another. In some recess of their mind they know they are becoming spiritually disoriented and yet they will not admit it even to themselves. I try to speak into their lives and show them in God's Word what is going on and what they should do. They tell me that they believe in God but when it comes to this area of their life they have decided to do it their way. They are bending the map. Maybe you have done it. Maybe you are doing it now.

I love what the author wrote about our need to be gazed upon in order to feel real. The further I move away from the gaze of the One who loves me the more wispy I become. And I find it fascinating that a lost hiker must first admit he is lost before he can be found. He must trust the map and resist the temptation to bend it. It is his only shot at being seen again and being set free from the fear that gnaws at his soul.

The Gospel is everywhere for those who have eyes to see.

Verse for Reflection:

Do not fear, for I am with you; do not anxiously look about you, for I am your God. I will strengthen you, surely I will help you, surely I will uphold you with My righteous right hand.

- Isaiah 41:10

Super Bowl? We're In!

Super Bowl XLV. There are truths that run so deep they ooze out of the earth and all that is in it. God made things in patterns so truth is always within our line of sight. The problem of course is we are so blind most of the time. I heard someone say the most common expression in heaven will be "of course." And what they mean is they will finally be able to see what was right in front of their face the whole time.

My friend is an avid Pittsburgh Steelers fan. He texted me to let me know "they" were going to another Super Bowl. He felt compelled to let me know because I am a Browns fan and he is a great sinner. The thing I found interesting was his identification with the football players. He is not and never has been a football player. He is not related in any way to any of the players. And yet, he feels a part of what he calls the Steeler Nation which is made up of a bunch of people like him who identify with a hundred huge burly men they do not know.

I told you there are truths that run deeper than any of us know. This is one of those truths. There is a longing in every human soul to iden- tify with someone or something greater than ourselves. The rest of the animal kingdom feels no such longing. It is unique to the human condi- tion and it is pervasive. If not sports, then movie stars, or rock stars, or artists or anyone that can lift us up. We are worshipers by nature. But it is more than that. We worship through identifying. We worship by somehow becoming "one" with them so what they do "we" do. Tim was telling me that in some way he was going to the Super Bowl.

In John 17, Jesus is praying and the disciples are hanging on every word. At one point He says something so profound that if they had not heard it with their own ears, they never would have believed. He said,

"I do not ask in behalf of these alone but for those also who believe in Me through their word; that they may all be one; even as Thou, Father, art in me, and I in Thee, that they also may be in Us; that the world may believe that Thou has sent me."

I have been reading some essays on the topic of our union with Christ. They were written by men who a friend affectionately calls "The Old Dead Guys." This is the ultimate union, the ultimate truth. There is nothing more deeply sewn into the fabric of the human soul than this longing to identify in such a way that we become one with someone who can truly and forever lift us up.

It is Jesus the Steelers Nation is longing for—even as "they" all go to the Super Bowl. And everyone who steps into heaven and sees the Son in all His glory will say, "Of course."

Verse for Reflection:

...so in Christ we who are many form one body, and each member belongs to all the others.

- Romans 12:5

Don't Ride It Alone

As far back as I can remember I have been involved in athletics. I enjoyed the competition, the camaraderie of a team, and the feeling of mind and body working together. I think I may have become addicted to endorphins too. I think those are the chemicals released into the body during physical exertion.

About 15 years ago I bought my first heart monitor. I loved that thing. I could ride my bike, target a heart rate and ride my little brains out. The heart rate monitor made it possible for me to work out as hard as I wanted to. I prided myself in being able to target a heart rate of say 172 and hold it there for an hour. I really thought I could ride as hard by myself as when I was riding with other people.

I've been watching the Olympics the last couple of weeks. Like everyone else I have watched as one world record after another has fallen. What I have come to realize is no one breaks a record when they are working out by themselves. These athletes are the best in the world. They aren't broken down athletes turned preachers. And yet, they are only at their very best when they are running, riding, swimming with others. That got me thinking about being a Christian.

Christians weren't made to live it alone. We were meant to be side by side with others running the same race. You not only make it less lonely for me, you make me better. Lately there seems to be an epidemic around me of lives exploding and marriages disintegrating. I think that happens in part because people head off with their heart monitor and think they can do just as well when they ride by themselves. Don't. You can't. The church is designed to be the group that rides with you, makes it safer, less lonely, and ends up spurring you on when you want to give up. All you loners out there, come on in and let's ride this one out together. One thing I have learned is that fellow riders are way better than a heart monitor.

Verse for Reflection:

As iron sharpens iron, so one man sharpens another.

- Proverbs 27:17

Cycling, Church, and Hanging on a Wheel

My son Jeremy is home for a couple of weeks. One of my great joys is riding bikes with him. He is a marvelous athlete so when the two of us go out together to ride it is an amazingly great and difficult ride. I have blogged about biking before. There is a slip stream behind a cyclist that makes an enormous difference.

Today Jeremy and I rode 37 miles at a demanding pace. We alternated being in front. After being in front for a mile I could hardly wait to slip in behind him and get some relief. Being in the slip stream means your front tire is about 6 inches from the rear tire of the one in front. If you drop farther than a couple of feet it is called "losing the wheel" and it means you are toast. If you and your partner were scooting along at say 25 mph and you lost his wheel you would drop to about 20 mph and still be working as hard as ever. To really rest would mean you would drop into the teens to catch your breath. You cannot lose the wheel of the rider in front of you.

Today's ride made me think of the church. I think when people drop out of church it is like losing a wheel. They think it is not that bad at first but after a while it really takes a toll. There is no where in the Bible where it talks about a Christian being without a church. I think because it is so hard to try to do it alone. I guess what I am saying is church helps you stay close to people moving in the same direction. In fact, if church is really working the way it should, then you will have people around you who are stronger than you are and pulling you around and people counting on you that you are stronger than hugging your wheel. And so it is. Whatever you do, don't drop back, stay home or lose a wheel. You may never make it home.

Verse for Reflection:

Two are better than one, because they have a good reward for their hard work. For if one of them should fall, the other one can raise his partner up. But how will it be with just the one who falls when there is not another to raise him up?

- Ecclesiastes 4:9-10

Pg. 13

The Race of Iron

There is an endurance race called simply "The Iron Man." The race includes a 2.4 mile swim in the ocean or a river, a 112 mile bike, and then a 26.2 mile run. The competition started in Hawaii but has now spread around. It is called the Iron Man because it is a test of will and one must have a will of iron to actually complete the race.

Yesterday I watched as my son completed the race. Actually it was a family affair. Karen, my daughter Rachel and my son-in-law Will, and Becca all ran around yelling encouragement to him during the different stages. It was blazing hot in Louisville and so even the 12-13 miles we walked to get to the different places took a toll. When my daughter Becca saw that Jeremy was struggling in the marathon she took off to run and walk beside him for 14 miles. I watched as other families did the same for other runners. People held signs and cheered. There were 2000 volunteers who helped with aid stations and traffic control. It really was amazing.

The last two miles Jeremy ran faster than the previous 24. He could sense the end and hear the cheers. And when he finally crossed the line the announcer yelled, "JEREMY COFFEY, YOU ARE AN IRON MAN." It was actually pretty emotional. It got me thinking about life and friends and the church. Life can be a struggle. In some ways you really don't know what kind of person you are until life gets hard.

I watched after the race the way the ones who finished treated each other. There is a deep respect. They all know something about each other that has to be true. They know when someone has finished that race that there is a toughness and tenacity and a strength that demands respect and they gladly give it.

It helps to have people around who are cheering. People who love you enough to want you to just keep going and putting one foot in front of the other when everything inside of you is screaming to stop. People who will cheer as you near the end of your journey. Many of you are like that for me. I want to be that for other people. But in the end there needs to be something inside of us that is willing to do the right thing. A desire to finish well that is stronger than the desire to take the easier way. What we do in the toughest of times tests our metal. Every man would like to know what he is made of. Yesterday my son Jeremy found out at least one ingredient that is in him in abundance...iron.

Verse for Reflection:

But they that wait upon the Lord shall renew their strength; they shall mount up with wings as eagles they shall run, and not be weary; and they shall walk, and not faint.

- Isaiah 40:31

100 Miles Has Me Thinking of Heaven

The Sports Impact ministry of our church got some of the serious bicycle riders together today to ride the 14 hills of the valley. It is very close to 100 miles up and down the hills leading in and out of the valley. I had to go. My wife and my daughter think I am crazy but I really love things like this. There are a few reasons. There is something immensely satisfying about doing something that is difficult to do. It is sheer joy to do something really difficult with some other people. There were around a dozen of us that gathered at the church at 7 a.m. this morning. Because we ride at different speeds we ended up breaking up into smaller teams. My team consisted of Leigh Atkins and Mark Gorman.

We had a blast. There is something that happens between people when they suffer together even if it is self induced suffering. King Henry had it right when he said, "He who sheds his blood with me this day shall be my brother be he ever so vile. And gentlemen now abed in England shall think themselves accursed and hold their manhood cheap that they were not here to fight on St. Crispen's Day." I think that quote is close. So, I love the challenge, I love the camaraderie and friendship that forms between fellow sufferers. But I also love one more thing. At the end of the ride when we are sitting around having a cold drink all the hardest parts of the ride are the things we laugh and joke about.

That reminds me of what heaven will be. Someday I will sit around and laugh at the hardest things in this life because all sad things will become untrue. At the church right now we are about to do some great stuff with adding campuses and a student ministry building. It will be a challenge. I will be asking people to sacrifice. Through it we will experience some of what I experienced today and so I can't wait. Thanks for coming along for the ride and I will see you at the top of the hill and we will laugh together.

Verse for Reflection:

Now may the God who supplies endurance and comfort grant you to have among yourselves the same mental attitude that Christ Jesus had, that with one accord you may with one mouth glorify the God and Father of our Lord Jesus Christ.

- Romans 15:5

Love is Not Simple

What do you think about illegal immigrants? How is that for an explosive question? As a Christian I have struggled with how I should feel. It is a tough question. This is the story of how I figured out how tough.

My friend Tom Randall spent 20 years in the Philippines. He loves the Filipino people. I mean he really loves them. You can tell by the way his face lights up every time he sees someone from Filipino descent or the way his countenance goes dark whenever there is news of a natural disaster on that side of the world. For 20 years his heart was knit to theirs and it is difficult for him to not feel Filipino himself most of the time.

Tom was also raised to be a patriot. A flag hung outside his house in the hardscrabble inner city of Detroit. His father fought in WW2 and his love for his country flowed into his son strong and sure. So I asked Tom about what he thought we should do about the illegal immigration problem particularly in the border states of the southeast. At first he gave what I would call the stock conservative answer: There is a way to become a legal alien; they are breaking the law; we should tighten the border and prevent the wave of people who are invading the borders.

But then I asked him what his answer would be if Mexico was filled not with Mexicans but with Filipinos. His face looked shocked at first and then a little hurt. Almost like I had done something unfair to him. He thought for a minute and then he said, "We should make their country so good that they will want to stay."

I wasn't trying to trap him. I was trying to get a perspective on how I should think about the problem as a Christian. God is a God of justice and justice is love evenly distributed. If you ever want to test that definition just try to treat your children differently. As soon as you do, the one who received less will yell, "It's not fair". And they will be right. I needed someone who loved Americans and illegal immigrants the same. Tom was the one person I knew who loved two nationalities exactly the same. Maybe that is why Tom's answer sounded as if it came straight from the mouth of Jesus. There is both a complexity and a simplicity to being a follower of Jesus Christ. The simplicity of loving people the same makes living in this world more complex. Do not settle for less. The struggle is real and unavoidable if you are a follower of the One who had no place to lay His head.

Verse for Reflection:

*We ought therefore to show hospitality to such men so that
we may work together for the truth.*

- 3 John 1:8

Listening to the Hope of the World

In June my youngest daughter went on a mission trip to the Dominican Republic. She is my child who is the most interested in missions. She asked a couple of weeks ago if some of the kids who went on the trip could come over to our house for what they were calling the "Upper Room." I said, "Sure."

So the other night they came. There were about 75 of them. They were like locusts. They ate everything we set out, drank everything, and then I am pretty sure I saw some teeth marks on the furniture. Anyway they ended up outside around our fire pit, all 75 of them.

Two students had guitars and began to lead worship. They sang and prayed for almost 2 hours. Toward the end I opened my bedroom window so I could hear. I looked out on 75 high school students gathered around a fire with their eyes closed and swaying together as they sang. They were singing Amazing Grace. As I listened I got goose bumps because I realized I wasn't just listening to high school students singing. I was listening to the hope of the world.

The world is always one generation from total collapse. Christianity is one generation from absolute extinction. Outside my bedroom window gathered a herd of teenagers who could have been out watching a movie or partying their brains out. Instead they stood under my window and sang Amazing Grace. So, the hope of the world gathered in my backyard the other night and I was thankful. I wanted to wake my neighbors and let them know that the next 20 years were going to be okay. I wanted them to know they could sleep well. God was not done with us yet. The fire has been lit in the next generation and so all is well. But I realized they were already awake. I just hope they had their windows open so they could hear the words... "I once was lost but now am found, was blind but now I see."

I don't know when I have felt so good about being up so late. Let them come and eat all I have as long as I can hear them sing as I lay in my bed and thank God that another generation has been lit and is burning bright.

Verse for Reflection:

Shout for joy to the Lord, all the earth. Worship the Lord with gladness; come before him with joyful songs. Know that the Lord is God. It is He who made us, and we are his; we are his people, the sheep of his pasture.

- Psalm 100:1-3

The Wedding That Waits

I think I understand why God has decided to have all of history end at a wedding. There is no greater avenue for love and joy and generosity and celebration to all meet together. After what I have experienced last night at the wedding of my dear daughter, I cannot wait until the day I stand with all of you at the wedding feast of the Lamb and experience the joy and the love our Father has planned for us since the beginning of time. Do you have any idea how generous a father wants to be on the wedding day? The supper of the Lamb will be beyond anything we can imagine. I can't wait to see all of you there.

Verse for Reflection:

Let us rejoice and be glad and give him glory! For the wedding of the Lamb has come, and his bride has made herself ready.

- Revelation 19:7

PART II
Letting Go, Letting God

Letting Go, Letting God

God has set forth a road map for each of our lives; however, it is up to us to listen to Him and follow the path He has set before us. Like the proverbial of the blind leading the blind, we cannot rely on ourselves to navigate all of the pitfalls that may occur in our lives. Only after we let go of our perceived control and rely totally on our Maker, trusting that He alone can guide us through all obstacles, will we be free to be as He made us to be.

Remember:

I praise you because I am fearfully and wonderfully made; your works are wonderful, I know that full well.

- Psalm 139:14

God works in mysterious ways and He has designed you specifically to carry out His plans. Trust in Him and He will provide. Here are some stories that help illustrate God's plan working in unimaginable ways.

Marble Heads

When I was in Florence I had the wonderful opportunity to see the sculpture of David by Michelangelo. It is situated in a hall so when you turn the corner you see it in all of its brilliance. David stands 17 feet tall. As I walked toward the sculpture I noticed other sculptures on the side. One is stuck inside my head. It is of a man who looks as if he is trying to pull himself out of the marble. It is one of the unfinished sculptures of Michelangelo, his torso partly free, his left arm reaching up to the block of marble that should have been his head. The arm is powerfully flexed but in all the years he hadn't made a lot of progress.

I was under the impression that he did it on purpose. It seems like he was showing us what he, as perhaps the greatest marble carver, could see. It was as if Michelangelo could see the man inside the marble and was knocking off what didn't belong.

Anyway, it was very moving to me partly because I feel much more like the guy trying to pull his head out of stone than I feel like David. I want to be like David and of course if I can't be like David the next best thing is for people to see me like David. David stands in a magnificent pose of strength and poise. He is a man who stands with his sling (and that is about his only article of clothing) and is completely relaxed in who he is and what he can do. I, on the other hand, am much more like the poor schlepp who is trying to pull his head out of a block of rock. My only hope is the Artist knows what He sees and He hasn't finished yet. Perhaps the man in the marble has struggled long enough to do it himself and will welcome the pain of the chisel.

I know I want to be free and I know my only hope lies with the One who not only holds the hammer and chisel but also knows exactly what I will look like with all the rock knocked off. So, here is a prayer for all of my fellow marble heads who long to be free:

Dear Father, Do what you must. Let the hammer fall and the chips fly. We want to be set free by Your grace and by Your power. We do not expect it to be painless but we long to smell the dust of progress deep inside these souls that are part living and part hard and lifeless as rock. Thanks for not leaving us unfinished. Amen.

Verse for Reflection:

So God created mankind in his own image, in the image of God he created them; male and female he created them.

\- Genesis 1:27

JoJo the Theologian

I have a dog named JoJo. Just so you know, I am not like George Foreman who named all his children George (4 sons and a daughter named Georgette...not kidding). I named my dog JoJo because she is a Jack Russel terrier and when she acted like a Jack Russel I wanted to remember she was my idea.

Anyway, I can't tell whether she is deeply religious and loves God or she is one of the new breed of virulent atheists who really hate God. During storms all the other dogs I have ever had run and hide under a bed especially if there are ear sleeping peals of thunder. Not JoJo. JoJo begs to go outside no matter how hard it is raining. Every time it thunders she runs back and forth in the yard looking up and barking her little brains out. She is a very strange dog. She is either running out there shouting to God and saying, "You are the greatest, and I am so pumped to hear You making all that noise. I'm JoJo and I just wanted to let You know I am exactly what You designed me to be. Look at me run and listen to me bark. Behold the Jack Russel You called forth from the foundation of the world." Or of course she is the deepest sinner dog who is out swearing and I just can't understand her.

I think she is doing the former. I remember reading C.S.Lewis and he said that man is the only wild animal. Every other animal acts exactly the way he was created to act. Only man is in rebellion. So, the next thunderstorm you might see me out in the yard running and yelling with JoJo with my face to the sky and the glory of God in my heart.

Verse for Reflection:

Let everything that has breath praise the Lord. Praise the Lord.

- Psalm 150:6

Fat Guy in a Skinny Body

I see commercials of people all the time who have lost a tremendous amount of weight. They have before and after pictures that are almost scary. The before picture they are all bloated and puffy and then the after picture is of a hotty that is almost unrecognizable. Of course, the advertisement is selling a product and the hope is that we will jump at the chance to become a hard body. I have met people who used to be really heavy and have lost weight. Sometimes they still see themselves as heavy. They feel like they are fat people in skinny bodies. They have been so used to being heavy all their lives it is difficult to believe they aren't fat anymore.

I am like that with grace I think. I am justified in the eyes of God because of what Jesus did on the cross. He was crushed so that I could be whole. He was blown apart so that somehow my fractured soul would come together. When God looks at me, He is filled with the same delight as when He looked at Jesus. "This is my beloved son in whom I am well pleased." God is talking about me. Wow! But I am so used to being a sinner. I am used to trying to justify myself by what I do. I am used to saying, "Listen, I know I am not perfect, but I am not all that bad. Look at me do something good. Look at me love a black man. Look at me let people out in traffic. Look at me get up early and pray."

I am constantly having to remind myself that I am saved by grace. I am loved because God loved Jesus and Jesus gave His life for mine. Jesus gave me His place in the heart of the Father. I need to quit being a fat guy in a skinny body. I need to quit being a sinner desperately trying to justify myself in the soul of a saint forgiven by the grace of God. So, today I will not justify myself by what I do. Instead I will remind myself of the wonder of a God who justified me by a sacrifice I can scarcely wrap my mind around and I will worship.

Verse for Reflection:

Therefore, if anyone is in Christ, the new creation has come: The old has gone, the new is here!

- 2 Corinthians 5:17

Chubby, Cold, and Dead

We have a bird feeder in our backyard for the first time. As the days get colder the activity around the feeder is picking up. The customers line up on the evergreen tree and then take their turn packing in as much as they can hold. I am a little worried though. I don't know a lot about birds but it seems like they should be heading south soon. I think it is the shortage of food that reminds them to pack their leisure suits and head to Florida.

I may be changing that with what seems to be a miraculous bird buffet. My fear is that one of these days I am going to see a bunch of chubby frozen birds gathered around my bird feeder and the guilt will be overwhelming. Actually, I won't suffer that much guilt. Who knows, I may use them as a prop for some obscure point in a sermon.

Here is my point. God designed birds to fly south. There are probably a bunch of really good reasons. I just recently mentioned King David in our Old Testament class. "In the times when kings go to war...David stayed home in Jerusalem." David quit doing what he was supposed to do and within a short time he jumped into bed with Bathsheba and the rest is history.

Sometimes I feel like taking the easy way. I don't feel like doing really wicked things right away, I just feel like I would like to take a break from doing the things I know I should. From now on, I will look at the bird feeder and imagine those chubby frozen carcasses and keep doing what I am designed by God to do. I suggest you do the same as we get ready for winter to come.

Verse for Reflection:

"For I know the plans I have for you," declares the Lord, "plans to prosper you and not to harm you, plans to give you hope and a future."

- Jeremiah 29:11

A Leash, the Law, and the Love of God

As far as dogs go, I think mine is pretty bright. Maybe not Ivy League smart but she would definitely be college bound. She rings a little bell to go outside, freaks out when we bring out the suitcases, and can play dead with the best of them. We were out walking the other day. Walking for her is one exquisite pleasure after another. If I ever get to the place where a walk gives me as much joy then I will absolutely have it made.

When my dog is at home her invisible fence keeps her out of a lot of trouble. She runs parallel with trucks and barks her little brains out. But when we are out walking I think she gets a little confused. I had her on a leash and it struck me that whenever a truck would go by she would strain and try to get to the truck. My leash is one of those retractable things (great invention) and so whenever a truck was coming I would have to start the process to reel her in and out of danger. Now my dog had no idea I was getting her out of danger. She would look up at me and I was sure she was swearing at me under her breath. She will never know how kind I was to her.

It got me thinking about the law of God. The psalmist says, "My delight is in the law of the Lord." Delight is a strong word. I don't know if I have ever looked at the law of the Lord and felt my heart leap. Maybe it is because I am more like my dog than I want to admit. If my dog really knew what I know about a truck traveling at 30 mph she would delight in the retractable leash and my effort to use it. So it is with God and me.

I have been reading the Bible differently lately. I read and then I delight and I thank God that He recognizes trucks that I might want to chase. So today, I walk with my dog as my God walks with me. My dog may only delight in the walk but I will delight in the Lord who is at my side and won't let me leave His.

Verse for Reflection:

Cast all your anxiety on him because he cares for you.

- I Peter 5:7

Stubborn Bushes and a Pang of Jealousy

Today is my day off. My wife asked me to help her around the yard. She wanted to transplant two bushes we had planted last year. I thought I could make quick work of it. I started to dig and 90 minutes later I was dragging the second bush to the new location. It was exhausting. I found it amazing how deep the roots had grown in a year. Roots are of course the key to how hard the plants were to dig up.

This past year those plants have gone through some serious weather. They went through the bone chilling winter, a rain soaked spring, and some serious summer storms. But throughout the year my two bushes have gotten what they really needed to grow. They received plenty of water and the nutrients in the soil were evidently exactly what the doctor ordered. Whatever was going on outside, these bushes were all about sinking their roots as deep as they could.

As sweat literally streamed off my body I was thinking about my own growth this past year. So many times I get side-tracked by what is going on all around me. I quit thinking about my roots. Like my bushes I think I have gone through some serious weather. Some of you have too, no doubt. But I have also had everything I need to sink my roots deeper into God.

As we close out summer I want to concentrate on growth. I want us all to ask God to help our roots to grow in such a way that a year from now we will be what Paul the Apostle called "steadfast and immovable." Because in all honesty, after only a year my bushes were very nearly steadfast and immovable. They made me jealous.

Verse for Reflection:

I pray that from his glorious, unlimited resources he will empower you with inner strength through his Spirit.

- Ephesians 3:16

Hurt People Hurt People

My daughter Becca and I visited an orphanage in Mexico. There is nothing quite like seeing and visiting with people who are running headlong toward Jesus. It seems like I meet more of them overseas than I do here. I guess that makes sense.

I remember talking to an Indian friend and mentioning how every person I ever met from India seemed wildly smart. My friend just looked at me slightly bemused and said, "It is only the smartest ones who ever get here." The educational system in India is built on a pyramid where at every level a test is administered and only the best and the brightest move on. It makes sense that there is a higher percentage of sold out Christians overseas. It is a little of the same logic.

Anyway, when we were at the orphanage one of the leaders was describing the difficulty facing each child who comes into the orphanage. She sighed and said almost matter of fact, "Hurt people hurt people." She didn't say it like it was profound. She said it like everyone should already know it. I didn't. To me it is a very profound truth. Think about it. Hurt people hurt people. What an awful truth. No wonder the world is such a mess. No wonder you are such a mess.

Assume that every human being is hurting. Every human being both a weapon and a victim then a weapon again and then a victim. All the way to Jesus. Jesus was just a victim. He was not a weapon. By absorbing the hurt He was offering to stop the cycle.

Isaiah said simply enough, "And by His stripes we are healed." Another profound truth. You and me healed. The cycle breaks because Jesus took both my guilt as a weapon and my pain as a victim. He heals and then says go and do likewise.

If hurt people hurt people then healed people should heal people. My guess is we heal the same way Jesus healed us and that is what the apostle Paul meant when he told us to fill up the suffering of Christ. Are you hurt or healed today? Let me be the first to tell you that you are healed. Today be a healer. You are no longer a weapon or a victim. You are a child of the Most High God.

Verse for Reflection:

The Spirit of the Lord God is upon Me, because the Lord has anointed me to preach good tidings to the poor; He has sent me to heal the brokenhearted, to proclaim liberty to the captives, and the opening of the prison to those who are bound.

- Isaiah 61:1

Biking, Jesus, and a New Friend

I was out riding my bike the other day. I was riding along a bike path during my lunch break. It is not too uncommon for me to see people from the church but I am cruising at around 20 mph and I have a helmet and glasses on so while I may recognize them they rarely recognize me. So, I zoom past and just say to myself, "Hey, I know them."

There is one place in my ride where I need to slow up to cross a neighborhood entrance. I slowed up and looked for cars and saw a lady from the church. I was riding slowly enough to recognize her and called her by name. She took a second and then recognized me and said, "Hi Joe." She said it in a way that made me come to a complete stop instead of racing on which is my habit especially at lunch.

She was riding with another young woman. Sue introduced me to her friend and said, "We were just talking. My new friend here is Muslim but she has been going to church and thinking about Christianity. She just asked me if there was anyone in our church who used to be Muslim she might be able to talk to about becoming a Christian. And right then you rode up." And then she introduced me to her friend and said, "This is our pastor. See, I told you God was working in your life." Her friend laughed and said, "I am not even trying and these things keep happening. All I have done is open my heart up to Jesus." It was a very cool moment.

I assured her that I could find someone and rode off smiling and shaking my head at how the God who created the cosmos out of nothing cares so much about 3 people riding bikes on a Wednesday afternoon. I went back to the church and told the story to the staff. Marshall Brandon laughed and told me that a good friend of his who was a former Muslim was coming to visit him Saturday and would be in church Sunday. God made that last move and I am pretty sure I heard Him say, "Check mate."

Verse for Reflection:

Do your best to present yourself to God as one approved, a worker who does not need to be ashamed and who correctly handles the word of truth.

- 2 Timothy 2:15

Incarnation: Lean Into It

My friend decided to move into the second worst neighborhood in Akron, Ohio. I don't know why he chose the second worst and not the worst. He was a fire fighter by trade but a Christian by vocation. He decided the city needed someone with flesh and blood to walk grace on the sidewalks. So he quit the fireman gig and moved downtown.

Soon after he arrived one of his new neighbors asked him what he was doing. Did I mention my friend is white? That was what caught his neighbor's eye. The real question was, "So, what is a middle-class white man doing in this part of town? You don't belong and you won't stay." My friend insisted he was there to stay so the neighbor simply said, "I will pick you up at 9 p.m. tonight. Be ready."

My friend was ready. The neighbor showed up right on time and the two walked to a neighborhood bar. When I say a neighborhood bar I mean there wasn't even a sign out front. If you were not from that neighborhood you would not even know it existed. My friend walked in as the first and only white man ever to set foot in that particular establishment. The neighbor waited for my friend to sit at the bar and as soon as he sat down the neighbor walked away. The bartender asked my friend what he wanted. He quickly ordered a beer and felt sweat begin to drip down his back. A young man came up and sat next to him. The young man began to regale my friend with stories of his latest sexual conquests. My friend could not have been more uncomfortable. Finally the young guy took a break and headed to the bathroom.

My friend got up and walked over to his neighbor. He said, "I want to leave." His neighbor asked why. My friend replied, "I am really uncomfortable. I want to leave now." His new friend looked up at him and said, "Lean into it." That was it. End of conversation.

My friend walked back to his seat and was stuck for another 40 minutes or so before his neighbor finally came over and told him they could leave. As soon as my friend got out to the car, he was ready to let his new friend have it, but the neighbor beat him to the punch, "Man–you want to come into this neighborhood and spread the love of Jesus. I just took you to where your lost sheep hang out. You gotta learn to lean into it if you are going to last. That guy was confessing to you, man. That is the closest you're going to get to getting that brother to church."

It was a good lesson for my friend. I love the incarnation. I am in love with the idea. But it really isn't incarnation unless from time to time you have to lean into it with all you got.

Verse for Reflection:

And we know that in all things God works for the good of those who love him, who have been called according to his purpose.

- Romans 8:28

A Reminder and a Warning

When I am on vacation I like to spend time reading. This was a particularly good vacation for me in that respect—I finished two great books and both had a profound impact on me.

The first book was "The Cross" by Martin Lloyd-Jones. It was a great reminder. This is an entire book devoted to unpacking a single verse of scripture, Galatians 6:14, "God forbid that I should glory, save in the cross of our Lord Jesus Christ, by whom the world is crucified to me and I unto the world."

One of the author's big points is that no one actually changes apart from the power of the cross of Jesus. As I thought about my own life and the lives of those I truly know on a deep level, I joyfully agreed. Real and lasting transformation can be traced right back to Jesus, what He did, and the overwhelming response of gratitude that kills the world's ability to control me, and enables me to die to the world.

Right after I finished the book I was driving down a road when a lady whisked by, leaving me with an excellent (but fleeting) view of her COEXIST bumper sticker. You know, the kind that screams, "Why can't we all just get along?" Suddenly, a car stopped in front of her—and she just LAID on her horn. When she pulled around the car, she shot a look that would have put Mrs. Potato Head's "angry eyes" to shame. Why can't we all just get along indeed? Martin Lloyd-Jones would say it will never happen apart from the cross, by whom the world is crucified to me and I to the world.

The other book I read was "Tempted and Tried," by Russell Moore. It's a book about temptation. The first chapter is titled, "Slaughterhouse Five." Cool title. The author compares the way we are tempted to the way cows are processed through a slaughterhouse. The handlers have developed techniques for keeping the cows calm by making the experience as similar to normal cow activity as possible. These days, instead of cattle-prods, they provide familiar touches, sights, and sounds, lulling the cows forward down the chute. The "blood room" at the end of the tunnel is the last thing they expect to find.

Here's the point: if you as a Christian are unaware of having an ongoing battle with active temptation, it's not because it isn't happening. You are in the gentle tunnel heading to the blood room. Very unsettling chapter. But vital reading, I think.

Pg. 33

As Christians we have a real enemy. Moore makes it clear that this enemy is ancient, patient, persistent, and personal. It was the personal part that stunned me. I guess I have always thought of temptation as being sort of passive. But that's not the way it works. The enemy of your life has someone actively assigned to you whose sole job is to poke around and design temptations that are custom fit just for you.

I have always known God had a plan for me personally. It makes sense that His sworn enemy would also have an agenda for me that was active, specific, and personalized.

Years ago I used to watch a television show called Hill Street Blues, about cops in NYC. In every show, after Sergeant Phil Esterhaus gave the morning briefing, he would end with the same warning I offer to you now, "Let's be careful out there." Indeed.

Verse for Reflection:

No temptation has seized you except what is common to man. And God is faithful; he will not let you be tempted beyond what you can bear. But when you are tempted, he will also provide a way out so that you can stand up under it."

- 1 Corinthians 10:1

The Weather Outside is Frightful

It is snowing outside as I write. I like snow. I like it even though it is dangerous to drive on, even though it is slick to walk on, even though it requires shoveling and scraping and makes my hands feel like wood. I am not sure why I like it so much. My daughter likes it because each flake is unique and beautiful in its own right. But I don't often take the time to look at individual flakes. I think it is because it covers my world in a white blanket. It makes the world quiet and a little softer. It also covers it in a single color.

It takes winter to make me ready to appreciate the single color of white. In the summer there are few things more beautiful than the green of a fairway on a cloudless day with the sky as blue as the ocean. Autumn brings a tapestry of colors that delights and surprises me every year. Winter comes and slowly turns the world brown. The leaves drop and the grass turns rusty and grey clouds cover the blue sky. But then the snow comes and the earth itself seems to pull the snow up to its chin like a quilt.

Like most things in my life, the snow makes me think of Jesus. When the snow drapes itself over the brown world I think of forgiveness. "Though your sins be as scarlet they shall be made white as snow" the prophet shouts. And so they are. My life all muddy and brown is made white and clean by the Son who loves me and shines brightest right here in the winter months. So, while the weather outside is frightful, the love of Jesus makes the weather in my soul better than ever.

Verse for Reflection:

Therefore, since we have been justified by faith, we have peace with God through our Lord Jesus Christ. Through him we have also obtained access by faith into this grace in which we stand, and we rejoice in hope of the glory of God.

- Romans 5:1-2

Weeds, Pride, Grace, and Rest

I like my lawn. I'm not crazy about it. But like most men I do like the nice striped lines that appear after I mow. There are some fairly stubborn weeds in my yard. By stubborn I mean they are pretty hearty. After years of enduring pesticides, they have become like the super heroes who have had some kind of nuclear toxin poured all over them and instead of curling up and dying like any normal living thing should, they acquire super human qualities.

Pride is a weed that grows deep down inside me. It is amazingly resistant to anything I throw at it. Someone years ago poured some toxin on it and instead of curling up and dying like any self-respecting weed should, it sucked the poison in, processed it and became some weird mixture of organic iron. Now my life's quest is to find the antidote, if that is the proper word for something intended to destroy and not preserve.

I remember hearing the story of a pastor who tried to battle his pride by volunteering at a soup kitchen. Early one morning he was mopping the floor and thought, "I am probably the only pastor in the city who is willing to mop the floor like this." After that thought he dropped the mop and walked out. That's the way pride mutates, adapts, and keeps growing.

The only antidote to pride in the entire universe is grace. Grace will kill pride. It is why deep down in places Christians don't talk about, we all hate grace. In order for grace to really make its way into my soul I have to admit I am helpless and hopeless and there is nothing that hurts more than that. But grace or pride are my only two options.

A.W.Tozer wrote that self-love is a heavy burden to bear. So it is. Jesus has the solution. He said, "Come to me all you who are weary and heavy laden and I will give you rest." Tired and weary of carrying the pride that is so hard to keep pumping up, I find myself staggering to Jesus for a little rest. What He gives me is the only rest He knows how to give–a rest laced with grace, and my pride feels it right away. Pride must curl up and die in order for me to lay my head on my Savior's lap.

I pray we will rest well today.

Verse for Reflection:

My soul finds rest in God alone; my salvation comes from him. He alone is my rock and my salvation; he is my fortress, I will never be shaken.

- Psalm 62:1-2

Glory!

God gives us gifts and sometimes they are almost indescribable. Moments where the thin fabric separating us from the eternal is pulled back and we see—if only for an instant—glory. It can happen without warning. The other day I experienced one of these moments while simply watching the face of my youngest daughter.

Becca is not yet 20 years old. Ever since she was a little girl she has felt the tug of God to participate in the movement of incarnation. She has wanted to give up, go to, and be with the children of the world. The ones that most need someone to love them. It is what her mother and I have raised her to do so every summer she begs us to let her go. And we do. Last summer it was Malawi, Africa. Malawi is poor even by Third World standards. She had no access to e-mail or telephone so for the better part of a month she dropped off the grid and we had no contact with her at all.

In "The Great Divorce," C.S. Lewis writes about people in heaven becoming more real and solid over time. Heaven is the most real place and according to Lewis we need to be in the presence for a while in order to become more real ourselves. When we picked up Becca at the airport she was more real. She has become as solid a 19 year old as I have ever known.

Becca is going back to Malawi again. But this time for most of the summer. We invited some of the people who supported her last year over to our house to hear a report of her trip. And to hear about the upcoming trip. She stood in the middle of our living room and spoke of her experiences in the dust and dirt of a tiny country in Africa. Finally she popped in a DVD that had been filmed at the orphanage the month before she had arrived. As the DVD began to play she would jump in with a name here and a story there. But after a while she just sat and watched with the rest of us. I quit watching the DVD and just watched her and that is when I saw it. Glory.

Becca sat with a smile on her face and her eyes brimming with tears as she watched the children she had grown to love flit across the screen. It was a compassion and a longing and a love so deep it could only come out in joy and tears.

I think that is the way the face of Jesus must look sometimes when He is watching us. So in some mysterious way it was the face of Jesus I caught a glimpse of that night. A character in one of Frederick Buechner's books had a similar experience and he described it like this:

"A light breeze blew from Wear that tossed the trees, and as I lay there watching them, they formed a face of shadows and of leaves. It was a man's green, leafy face. He gazed at me from high above. And as the branches nodded in the air, he opened his mouth to speak. No sound came from his lips, but by their shape I knew it was my name. His was the holiest face I ever saw. My very name turned holy on his tongue. If he had bade me rise and follow to the end of time, I would have gone. If he had bade me die for him, I would have died. When I deserved it least, God gave me most. I think it was the Savior's face itself I saw."

Every once in a while the fabric is pulled back and God gives us a glimpse. Look for it. He who has eyes to see let him see. Glory!

Verse for Reflection:

Then Jesus came to them and said, "All authority in heaven and on earth has been given to me. Therefore go and make disciples of all nations, baptizing them in the name of the Father and of the Son and of the Holy Spirit, and teaching them to obey everything I have commanded you. And surely I am with you always, to the very end of the age."

- Matthew 28:18-20

PART III
An Astounding Love

An Astounding Love

God knows you inside and out. He knows all of your flaws and blemishes, but He loves you regardless. He has created us and said "it is good," sent Jesus Christ as a sacrifice to die on the cross to set us free from our sin, and He still is reaching out to us no matter how hard we try to push Him away.

Verse for Reflection:

But in all these things we overwhelmingly conquer through Him who loved us. For I am convinced that neither death, nor life, nor angels, nor principalities, nor things present, nor things to come, nor powers, nor height, nor depth, nor any other created thing, shall be able to separate us from the love of God, which is in Christ Jesus our Lord.

- Romans 8:37-39

God has provided us with an unrelenting love that rightfully should astound us all. Even with the vast abundance of sin in our lives, He has not nor will He ever abandon us. In this chapter, there are stories about being worse than you would ever want to admit and yet loved more deeply than you ever thought imaginable.

Looking Through a Key Hole

Well, John McCain has chosen his running mate. Soon we will know more about Sarah Palin than we ever wanted to know. We are already hearing about what she has not done. Soon, we will hear about everything she wished she hadn't done. Going into politics is like walking through customs at the airport. It may begin slowly but it could very easily progress to a full out cavity search. Sorry for that image.

Jean Paul Sartre, the existentialist philosopher, wrote a short story that captured why he was an atheist. In the short story he was spying on someone through a key hole. He felt a thrill as he watched them in part because he was getting completely unfiltered information about them. Then he heard a noise and realized that someone was looking through a key hole at him. It was God. Sartre said if God exists then He gets completely unfiltered information about us. For Sartre that was the most horrifying thought ever.

Many of us would never think about running for public office because it is just a taste of this. All of us like to present ourselves to people on our terms. If my unfiltered thoughts would somehow spew themselves into this blog it would be the last time I ever opened a computer. But we have a problem. We have a deep fear of people really knowing what is going on deep down inside of us. We filter our presentation of ourselves even to our closest friends. But we also have this terrible need to be loved. And love is only as powerful as true knowledge of a person.

And here is the wonder. God does look through the key hole at my life. He has completely unfiltered information about me. And yet, God loves and that is the greatest mystery of all. That is why God's love is so much greater than we can imagine because God knows. He knows and He still loves. That may be something Sarah Palin may need to be reminded of before this is all over. It is something that is my joy to remind you of today.

Verse for Reflection:

By this we shall know that we are of the truth and reassure our heart before him; for whenever our heart condemns us, God is greater than our heart, and he knows everything.

- 1 John 3:19-20

On Rain, Lasagna, and God's Gifts

I am sitting here looking out my office window. It is streaked with rain. Yesterday was absolutely gorgeous. The sky was a deep blue, the temperature perfect, the sun shining until it finally winked as it slipped under the horizon in the evening. Why is it I describe yesterday as gorgeous and today I sit and look out my window and sigh? Better question- God had a completely blank canvas when He decided to create this world. Why did He decide to not just make seasons but also here in Ohio to make days so wildly different that they in themselves seem like seasons.

God created us as the pinnacle of His creation. He created us with all kinds of needs, some we know and recognize and some we don't. The psalmist says, "God gives to His beloved in his sleep." That was his way of saying that God is giving to us all the time even when we don't recognize what He gives as a great gift. Last night I ate lasagna. It was leftover lasagna. Now with two of my three kids gone lasagna lasts longer than it used to. A little too long if you know what I mean. I hate to waste stuff but I have to say I was glad that last night we finished off the lasagna. I need some variation in my diet. God made me like that.

That got me thinking about the rain. I was sitting here and wishing today was more like yesterday. But what if I really need the rain? What if I need the rain as much as the grass or the flowers? That of course led me down the road to other things I avoid or don't like. What if all my pain and discomfort are like little vitamins or brussels sprouts (wow, I really hate those things)? I guess as I sit looking out my rain streaked window I am thankful that there is a God in charge of everything who loves me more than I can imagine and knows more about what I really need than I ever will. So, today I am thankful for the rain and for a God who calls me His Beloved and gives to me in my sleep. Sleep well my friends even as the rain falls...especially as the rain falls.

Verse for Reflection:

But now thus says the Lord who created you, O Jacob, and he that formed you, O Israel, fear not: for I have redeemed you, I have called you by your name; you are mine. When you pass through the waters, I will be with you; and through the rivers, they shall not overflow you. When you walk through the fire, you shall not be burned; neither shall the flame kindle upon you.

- Isaiah 43:1-2

Jesus and Breaking the Speed Limit

I speed. I don't mean that I am a pedal to the metal kind of person. I am not a speed demon. I just speed...a little...all the time. I drive right around 3-4 mph over the limit. It is not enough to feel badly about. What is interesting is that it is not even enough to make much of a difference in how quickly I get where I am going. To be honest I haven't thought about it enough to come up with the deep reason I am doing it. This is what I do know. I try to rationalize it. I say to myself, "This really isn't that bad and isn't really wrong." And then I see a policeman. Immediately I look down at my speedometer, take my foot off the gas, and look feverishly in the rear view mirror until I can no longer see him. It's amazing I haven't crashed while looking back hoping not to get a ticket.

The law of the Lord is like a light, scripture says. The law shines and shows me what I am. So it is. There is no excuse, no rationalization, no escaping the law. It is what it is. This is the thing. The law shows me as worse than I think I am. If it is true with driving just think of what it is like in all the other parts of my life. So, once again I am reminded of Jesus and of grace. Today, as I drive home (within the speed limit) I will remind myself that I am worse than I have ever wanted to admit and more deeply loved than I ever dared to imagine. Even a ticket will just remind me of the wonder of grace today.

Verse for Reflection:

Each time he said, "My grace is all you need. My power works best in weakness." So now I am glad to boast about my weaknesses, so that the power of Christ can work through me.

- 2 Corinthians 12:9

Two Pleasures

I was reading C.S.Lewis last night. That guy can write. He was writing about pleasure. There are at least a couple of different pleasures we enjoy. One is need pleasure. That is what we enjoy when we are really thirsty and someone hands us a cold glass of water. The other is appreciative pleasure. That is what happens when we are walking along perfectly content and then smell a wood fire coming from a chimney and we are struck with a simple and profound pleasure. I think when I am walking and the smoke of a chimney hits me I always smile. There is some kind of childhood yearning that wells up inside of me.

Anyway, these are two kinds of pleasure. It made me think of my relationship with God. I think of the psalmist who writes, "As the deer pants for the water so my soul longeth after you, O Lord." I feel that way quite a bit. That is need and while my physical thirst can be slaked by a tall glass of water my longing for God will never be completely satisfied in this life or the next. I was made to be dependent on God. But my relationship with God needs to also include the other pleasure–the appreciative pleasure.

I want to be captured by the beauty and power and glory of God. There must be times when I am walking and the pleasure of His presence thrills me and even surprises me. So, I am not going to be content to just be a one pleasure guy. I think God knows I need Him. I want God to know that there is a deeper pleasure He gives me.

Maybe it is what I see with my daughter and her new born son. Right now Liam needs her and that is all he feels. It is enough for her to be needed and she understands his need as love. But there will come a time when it will be nice when Liam does more than just need his Mom. It will be a time when he starts to run out the door and then stops and comes back and looks his mom in the eye and says, "Thanks Mom. I love you and I think you are the most beautiful mom in the world." And my daughter's heart will melt. That is the way I want God to feel today as I turn around and tell Him not just how much I need Him but how I do love Him.

Verse for Reflection:

Like newborn babies, crave pure spiritual milk, so that by it you may grow up in your salvation, now that you have tasted that the Lord is good.

- 1 Peter 2:2-3

Pg. 44

Becca and Her Car

My wife and I gave our 16 year old daughter a car the other night. Becca had been sharing a car with her grandmother and we thought eventually that would get really complicated so we bit the bullet and presented her with a 2001 Pontiac.

I don't like to give any big gift without some drama so this is what I did. I had her drive her grandmother's car to The Porch (the high school ministry). Karen and I drove the Pontiac up to church and then moved Nana's car. Becca came out of The Porch and thought the car had been stolen so she called us.

We told her to come to the front of the church so I could have a talk with her. I told her as we walked toward the car that Nana didn't want her to drive her car anymore. I asked her what she did to get this kind of reaction from her grandmother. Becca was rocked. She finally said, "I moved the tilt steering wheel. Would that have done it?" Sometimes it is pitiful how easily my kids are taken it in, but there is a certain sweetness to it.

Finally, I said to her, "Okay, Mom has to drive Nana's car home so why don't you drive this one" and I handed her the keys and pointed her to the Pontiac. She hesitated, looked at me, looked at the car, looked back at me, and then finally started yelling and jumping and overall responding just the way I hoped a 16 year old would respond to her first car. It was great. I like the curve. I liked bringing it low before it went crazy high.

It is like the Gospel. Joe, you are a sinner, really, seriously, a sinner and it is really, really bad. Then God says, "So, since you are a sinner and in desperate trouble, why don't you take this," and God points me to the cross. Gratitude is increased when the really good news follows really bad news. So, let your heart, like mine, be like a 16 year old. Let us leap and shout and search the face of God with wonder and expectation as it slowly dawns on us how much our Father loves us. I want to love God with the same ferocity that my Becca loved me when she wrapped her arms around me in front of a white Pontiac and said, "Daddy, I love you."

Verse for Reflection:

Here is a trustworthy saying that deserves full acceptance: Christ Jesus came into the world to save sinners—of whom I am the worst. But for that very reason I was shown mercy so that in me, the worst of sinners, Christ Jesus might display his unlimited patience as an example for those who would believe on him and receive eternal life. Now to the King eternal, immortal, invisible, the only God, be honor and glory for ever and ever. Amen.

- 1 Timothy 1:15-17

Turning My Heart Toward Him

I journal as a discipline. It actually helps me focus when I am praying. It also ruthlessly points out when I am talking to God way too much about me. Yesterday I caught myself having a monologue about myself with God in the room so I stopped. I thought I would share what I wrote then because it profoundly changed the way I experienced God and the rest of the day.

"Too much me. Lord, You are the one who is sovereign. You know what You want to accomplish, who You are working on. You are the author and perfecter of faith. You created the cosmos, as I read yesterday, You formed the sun and moon and the stars...made all things and called them good. You made the rivers and the mountains, the ecosystem (which I am completely impressed by), the sky and the seasons... and it was good. You made a place for the one in Your image, the garden and placed man in the middle and it was very good. You walked with him there in the garden and then in Your goodness you made for him a companion... Isha (Hebrew for woman. "Ish" is man), and the two reflected the community of the trinity. Your nature in flesh. And they broke Your heart. And we have been breaking Your heart ever since. We have loved others, given our deepest affections, made them our heart's desire and they have come back to abuse and enslave us. And You, like a jealous lover, came to rescue us (Hosea) and moved heaven and earth to get us back. You gave us yourself on the cross to pay for the infidelity of Your bride and You ask us again and draw us to Yourself. So I come to experience You as King and Savior and Friend and Love."

Reminding myself of the greatest story and the greatest movement of love the world has ever known changed my heart and my focus. I hope it does the same for you today.

Verse for Reflection:

And he said to all, "If anyone would come after me, let him deny himself and take up his cross daily and follow me.

- Luke 9:23

Water, Water Everywhere
and Not a Drop To Drink

We have a well at our house. That means the water that comes in runs through a softener before coming out the tap. I looked at the amount of softener I put in and decided it would be better for my family to not drink all that salt so we order our water from Distillata. Usually it comes like clockwork. This past week there was a glitch and instead of getting our water every two weeks they missed a delivery and didn't deliver for four. It was interesting how it impacted us.

Our house became a little desert. We wandered around with rags on our heads and our lips cracked checking every day to see if the bottles had been delivered. It wasn't quite that bad but you understand. There was a time when all water was good water. When we drank out of the tap or out of a hose. But now with all the stuff we have found in water we have turned to purified water. I think it is probably a good thing.

It seems we have done the exact opposite with spiritual things in our country. We used to get spiritual water only out of the Bible. It came out cold and pure. Now we look for spiritual advice from everyone from Oprah to the latest pseudo spiritual novel. I guess my advice for the day is to quit drinking out of every spiritual hose and let's get back to the stuff that came deep from the heart of God and was bottled before the foundation of the earth. In our spiritual world there really is water, water everywhere but so much of it contains the things that will eventually make us really sick. So today, go to your bookshelf and take out the Bible and imagine your dry lips wrapping around a bottle of ice cold purified water and let the God who loves you quench the thirst of your soul.

Verse for Reflection:

As the deer pants for streams of water, so my soul pants for you, my God. My soul thirsts for God, for the living God. When can I go and meet with God?

- Psalm 42:1-2

Immanuel-The Breakable God

I have been thinking that the Christmas season is a wonderful time... for most of us...most of the time. It is precisely because it is so great most of the time that it can be such an incredibly difficult time as well. This got me thinking about pain during the holidays. There is tremendous warmth and goodness during this time but pain peaks as well doesn't it? It should not surprise us.

The shepherds watched as the angels sang of great joy. They ran into Bethlehem, saw the Child, and then laughed and sang their way back to the sheep. God had come and they were no longer alone. But when God came there was also a dark side to all the joy. At Christmas we celebrate Immanuel, God with us. It is the time when God became breakable. Christianity is the only religion in the world that teaches that we can actually hurt God and we did. Hurting God became possible because of Christmas.

Christmas does not give me the reason for suffering and pain. When suffering happens there are usually two possible responses. Some will think that God wasn't paying attention. That God is an absent God and doesn't really care. The other response is that God is vindictive and is punishing people for their decisions and their sin. Christmas forces us away from both those answers. The fact that God became Immanuel means that He is not absent. He is not a God who ignores our pain but instead has entered in. We may not know why suffering happens but as Christians we have a God who is willing to take the medicine Himself. I will never suffer something He was not willing to suffer.

He is not absent.

The other truth that comes out at Christmas is that Jesus came to pay for our sin. That means that suffering is not because God is vindictive. If you are hurting this season I write this for you. If you are in pain then it is at Christmas you can be reminded that God came to be with you right in the middle of that pain. If your life is going well and you are looking forward with great anticipation to a joy filled time around a feast with friends and family, remember it is Immanuel who has given you joy. Either way, Christmas is a time of wonder. The infinite became finite, the immortal became mortal, the omnipotent became breakable...for you...with you.

Verse for Reflection:

The Word became flesh and made his dwelling among us. We have seen his glory, the glory of the one and only Son, who came from the Father, full of grace and truth.

- John 1:14

There is Evening and
There is Morning

Years ago I remember seeing a preacher named E.V.Hill deliver a sermon entitled "I Have Been Through the Night." E.V. Hill is an African American preacher who was considered by some to be the best preacher of his time not just for what he said but how he said it. I still remember him saying at one point, "I have laid my hands on tumors and seen them shrivel up and disappear and I have laid my hands on my wife and watched as God took her to glory, I have been through the night." E.V. had seen some people get healed and yet the one he probably wanted healed more than any other was not and God took her to glory.

I write that now because while I am grateful that God has been gracious to my family in allowing my dad to be with us a little longer, I also know there are plenty of you out there who have been through the night. When my little brother died I remember thinking that if God wants credit every time someone gets better He should be prepared to get the blame every time someone does not. Now 20 some years later I still don't know why God does what He does. Out of all the questions I can ask God, the why question is the one that burns and yet it is the why question that in the long run may not matter at all.

Suppose God could explain in his divine calculus why it was better for my brother to die at 20 and for my father to live at 76. Even if I could understand it, I would still miss my brother the same and still be rejoicing in that my dad was going to celebrate another Christmas with us. I guess I am writing this to let you all know who are going through the night, that I still feel for you. I don't think there are easy answers and please don't think that God answers our prayers because we are clergy and not yours.

I remember being mad at God for a while after my little brother died. I ended up really missing God. I also remember reading a psalm where the psalmist said, "Two things I know of you, two things have I heard. That you O God are strong and that you O Lord are loving." The psalmist spoke truth into my life in the midst of the night during the loss of my brother and he speaks the same truth into the joy of the morning now with my dad.

Verse for Reflection:

Do you not know? Have you not heard? The Lord is the everlasting God, the Creator of the ends of the earth. He will not grow tired or weary, and his understanding no one can fathom. He gives strength to the weary and increases the power of the weak.

- Isaiah 40:28-29

Scars

The human body has a memory system designed especially for pain. The system is called scarring. Scars tell a story of something painful that has happened. Small or large they still speak of pain many years later. Every scar tells a story. I have a scar on my head. This is the story.

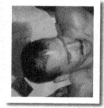

I was in the Dominican Republic building an orphanage. We were digging a trench for drainage around the foundation. One of the high school students was using a pickaxe to dig out the section closest to the concrete foundation. I told him it looked a little dangerous and he ought to let me do it. I took a mighty swing with the pickax, which bounced off a piece of hidden rebar, recoiled, and struck me right in the head. I staggered back and sat down on a stack of blocks. Blood began to pour down my forehead. I am probably the only person you've heard of with a self-induced pickax wound.

I had been working with two Dominican men. They ran over and did something I will never forget. Moses put his thumbs in the wound to staunch the bleeding as Montero put both hands on my face and began to pray. I thought how different their response was from my own. My immediate response is always to try to fix whatever is broken or find someone who can. In this case it would eventually be my surgeon friend Art who was also on the trip. But Montero decided to go right to the top, and he did so without hesitation. It is a lesson I am still trying to learn.

That is the story of the scar on my head. It's a scar that reminds me of my own frailty and of Montero's faith.

Every scar tells a story.

The scars that Jesus bears on His body tell a story. Stop and let that sink in. Jesus Christ, Son of God, has scars on His hands and His feet and His side. Scars. The body does not forget certain pain. Jesus' body remembers.

There is a song that says, "My name is written on the palm of His hand." True enough. My name as well as yours caused the scar. It is a wound that I should have but I don't.

Every scar tells a story. The scars on the body of Jesus tell the greatest story of all. It is the story of grace. His scars gave us life.

Verse for Reflection:

Now faith is being sure of what we hope for and certain of what we do not see.

Pg. 50

- Hebrews 11:1

The Fondness of God

Maybe it is the wedding but I have found myself thinking more and more about love. Particularly I have been captivated by the love of God lately. I find myself looking forward to getting up every morning. I remember hearing Brennan Manning tell the story of his Irish uncle who was standing looking at a sunset. Brennan went up and stood beside him and his uncle smiled and said simply, "My Heavenly Father is very fond of me."

I guess I have been feeling more and more like that since it struck me that God created everything for the pleasure of Adam. I sit in my chair in the morning with my coffee and look out at the sunrise and think, "My Heavenly Father really is very fond of me." It is a very cool way to start my day.

There are only four ways to motivate me to change...guilt, fear (those two are pretty closely connected), pride, and love. Maybe for the first time or at least for the first time in a long time, I feel like I am being changed by love. I don't know how long this feeling will last but I have found myself smiling every morning as I sit listening and talking to a God who pulled the sun up on a string just to show me.

Verse for Reflection:

But God demonstrates his own love for us in this: While we were still sinners, Christ died for us.

- Romans 5:8

A Single Drop

Have you ever noticed how certain movies play on cable over and over again? Right now we are cycling through the Tolkien classic, "The Lord of the Rings." Few movies are as good as the books they are based on and "The Lord of the Rings" is no exception. For example, the movie left out the part where the hobbits returned to their beloved Shire. That was practically the climax and it was not in the movie. The evil Saruman had desecrated and destroyed the beauty of the Shire. Sam Gamgee was particularly crestfallen until he remembered a small box the Lady Galadriel had given him. Inside the box was fine dust that she had collected from her garden. As Sam began to replant the Shire he carefully placed a single grain of dust onto every sapling. Almost overnight the Shire exploded in beauty and magnificence. There was such power in the box that every grain of dust was precious.

Ever since I first read that account something has been stirring in my soul. The old hymn writers often wrote of the power of the blood of Jesus and I wonder if that is what's stirring deep down inside me at the telling of this strange little story about hobbits. My soul torn asunder, Saruman running around cutting and slashing for years on end until all the beauty and wonder is gone. And then a single drop, less than a drop, of the precious blood of Jesus falls on the wasteland of my soul. The wonder of the drop is that not only does it remove the pain of the destruction, but in its place it leaves a treasure beyond reckoning.

Sam placed the grains of dust and waited. This is how regeneration of the Shire is described:

"Spring surpassed his wildest hopes. His trees began to sprout and grow as if time was in a hurry and wished to make one year do for twenty. In the Party Field a beautiful young sapling leaped up; it had silver bark and long leaves and burst into golden flowers in April. It was indeed a mallorn, and it was the wonder of the neighborhood. In after years, as it grew in grace and beauty it was known far and wide and people would come long journeys to see it."

There was no destruction Saruman could do that a single grain of dust could not undo. And so it is with the precious blood of the Lamb. There is no damage to your soul that cannot be undone by a single drop of that blood. I don't know what a mallorn is. Tolkien was always making up names for things. But my heart leaps when I think that Jesus does the same thing. He has a new name waiting for me. A single drop and my soul explodes in grace and beauty and I will be called by my new name.

Maybe I am a mallorn after all. And maybe you are too. It only takes a drop.

Verse for Reflection:

Whoever has ears, let them hear what the Spirit says to the churches. To the one who is victorious, I will give some of the hidden manna. I will also give that person a white stone with a new name written on it, known only to the one who receives it.

- Revelation 2:17

A Whistle to Follow

As long as I can remember my dad has been a whistler. He is not a hummer, he whistles.

Dad has a normal whistle that he uses when he is just walking around. Those are usually hymns. He also had a whistle to call us home when we were kids. That was amazing. He didn't have to put his fingers in his mouth, he just pursed his lips in a certain way and it sounded like a siren.

I always thought I would be able to do that someday. Actually I thought it happened automatically when someone became a dad. Sadly, I never mastered the amazing siren whistle.

This past week I have been on a bicycle ride from Cincinnati to Cleveland to raise money for some justice and mercy ministries. We rode 400 miles in 5 days. As we got close to our church we gathered more and more riders. There was a crowd gathered outside our church to cheer and welcome us home. When we got within a couple of blocks I heard it. The whistle. It made me smile. I couldn't see my dad yet but I knew he was there waiting for me.

I'm 52 years old and I still recognize the whistle of my dad calling me home. I think in some way I have been following that whistle all of my life. I followed that whistle right into the ministry. There are few things more precious than having a father who lives a life worthy of following. I have had that my whole life.

If your father was not one worthy of following there is still hope. The whistle may not be as loud. It may not be audible at all. But the Father calls you just the same.

When the disciples asked Jesus to teach them to pray, He started by telling them what to call God. He told them to call Him Father. It was His way of telling them the faint whistle they had been hearing their whole life was His.

If you sit long enough in the silence of the morning you can hear it too. I hear it nearly every morning when I open the pages of my Bible. I cannot see Him but I can hear Him and I know He is there.

It is a whistle worthy of following.

Verse for Reflection:

See what kind of love the Father has given to us, that we should be called children of God; and so we are. The reason why the world does not know us is that it did not know him.

- 1 John 3:1

Pg. 54

PART IV
Hidden Treasures

Hidden Treasures

God has placed hidden treasures all around us to remind us of His love and to also remind us of how we should love Him. If we open our eyes to the every day blessings that surround us, we would realize God is always with us and is impacting our world through the very people and situations to which we have become numb. By placing God in His rightful place atop the priorities in our lives, we start to see the awesomeness of all the hidden treasures He has seemingly hidden right in front of our faces.

Verse for Reflection:

For where your treasure is, there will your heart be also.

- Matthew 6:21

Recognizing the expanse of all that God has given us is important; however, as we start to acknowledge the veiled blessings that He bestows upon us daily, we may fall victim to another common misstep, displacing our Lord with one of His gifts. If we are not careful God can be easily supplanted by the very blessings He's given us, whether it be your money, career, or even your family. The stories that follow provide a myriad of examples showing the danger of what happens when the "treasures" that we value so dearly in our lives find themselves between you and the best treasure of all, a relationship with God the Father.

Do You Feel Lucky?

There is a scene in a movie I have watched where a character says, "I must be the most unlucky person in the world." The other character decides to educate him. The wise character says something like this, "You only say you are unlucky because you didn't realize how lucky you were yesterday. You thought yesterday you were just normal and now that things have taken a turn all of a sudden you feel unlucky. If today you are unlucky then every day up to this one you were very lucky so you should feel like you are a lucky person." I thought the scene was fascinating.

Sometimes people come into my office and they think their life is very, very bad. They feel "unlucky." What they don't know is someone has just left my office that had a much worse situation. What is interesting to me is the attitudes people have. Most people think their attitude is a result of what is going on outside of them.

After watching people for a long time I don't think that is the case. Attitudes seem to be based on expectations more than experiences. I sit with some people who are going through horrific experiences and yet they have an attitude laced with joy. Others fight the pull of bitterness and depression. I have been thinking more and more about the Gospel. It is the Gospel that helps me move everything in my life into the category of grace. If it is hell I deserve (and make no mistake, I do deserve it) then there isn't anything that can happen to me where I cannot say, "I had that coming." If it is grace I am given then there isn't a single good thing that happens where I cannot say, "Wow, I did not deserve that." I have to believe the Gospel is designed to change the way I experience every single thing in life. When I live by grace there isn't a day that goes by where I don't feel lucky.

Verse for Reflection:

Do not be anxious about anything, but in every situation, by prayer and petition, with thanksgiving, present your requests to God.

- Philippians 4:6

More Than a Game

I just talked to a soccer coach who coaches at a Christian school. The program is an excellent one and they are a pretty accomplished bunch. Anyway, we were talking about a great win they recently had against a rival school. He told me that the team decided instead of gathering after a game and forming a circle and praying together they would do something different.

The players decided after shaking hands with their opponents they would circle back and pick out one opposing player to pray with. They go up to the player and say,"Hey, really good game. I know this will sound kind of strange but would it be ok if I just prayed with you?" I don't know what your high school athletic experience was like but this is stunning to me. The coach told me the response has been unbelievable. Every game brings him to tears and I can see why.

It impacts how his team plays since they know at the end of the game they will be targeting someone to pray with. One player said the kid he asked said, "Do you mean like the Lord's Prayer or something?" And the student said, "No, not really. I just want to pray for you that God would be real in your life." And so he did. And I think God could hardly be happier. These are kids who play the game hard and well but in the end they know that it is more than just a game.

There is something bigger going on. I was thinking how that would change the way we live. Would it change the way you drive if you knew you would be putting your arm around someone and asking if you could pray for them at the next rest stop. Would it change the way you do business or deal with a fellow employee? Anyway, the whole conversation inspired me. I am glad there are kids like that in the world. I am glad to know the story. This is the first time in a long time I have wanted to be more like a 17 year old than someone my age.

Verse for Reflection:

Now may the God who supplies endurance and comfort grant You to have among yourselves the same mental attitude that Christ Jesus had, that with one accord YOU may with one mouth glorify the God and Father of our Lord Jesus Christ.

- Romans 15:5

The Itch

Chlorine makes me itch. I have been swimming lately in order to mix up my workout some. On swim days I itch. One of the things that bugs me is I over-scratch. I find that scratching an itch really feels good. It feels so good I continue to scratch and it is only when I quit scratching that I realize instead of an itch I now have pain. There are times when I know I am over-scratching and I still do it. I do the same with eating sometimes. I am hungry so I eat but then eating feels so good I over eat. I am hoping you can relate and this isn't just a weird confession.

Lately I have been wondering why. I think it is because I am not home yet. I mean the itch reminds me that something is not quite right here in this world. Don't get me wrong, right now my life is pretty great with my first grandchild and all. Did I mention I am a grandfather? So, life can be good and yet something is not quite right. It is an itch? And then even the scratching goes over the top and doesn't do the trick. There is an itch in my soul. I have a longing and if I try to scratch it with anything in this world my tendency is always to over-scratch.

I see it all around me. It can be people with their jobs or with money or with over the top vacations or parents way too much into their kids. Did I mention I am a grandfather? And there is the itch and the scratch and the reminder that I am not home. I was made for God and the itch in my soul will only go away when I am at last with the One for whom I was created. Until then I will be reminded with every itch of what my soul really longs for and will be grateful for a Savior who paid the price for me to find my way home.

Verse for Reflection:

Therefore, since we are surrounded by such a great cloud of witnesses, let us throw off everything that hinders and the sin that so easily entangles. And let us run with perseverance the race marked out for us.

- Hebrew 12:1

Hell and Celebrity Rehab

I watch a show called "Celebrity Rehab." I am not even going to try to justify it or say I was channel surfing and happened upon it. I watch the show okay? Wow, I am glad I got that off my chest. Anyway, the show is about celebrities who are in rehab trying to make it to sobriety. Their guide is Dr. Drew, who really does seem pretty gifted. I watch as these poor souls struggle to break free from their addictions. Some things, like alcohol and opiates result in a quick disintegration. The lives of these celebrities have completely come apart due to their addiction and they have destroyed nearly all relationships in the process. They are isolated and still craving the substance that has made them so lonely.

They sometimes describe their condition as being in hell. I think in some ways they are right. God made us for Himself. Anything I put in His place is bound to be less than what I need there in my soul. I will demand more and more of it until it begins to make me come apart at the seams. The problem with most of our addictions is they are slow acting. The man with the job that keeps his mind whirling through the night doesn't realize his addiction. The woman who sits up and worries all the time about her children thinks of herself only as a good mom. But if I take these and extrapolate them out hundreds or even thousands of years what will be left of that person?

I watch Celebrity Rehab and I see people who desperately need God. They are going to replace one habit with another. Cocaine for Cheetos. What then? Then I think of all the people who are addicted to the slow acting things like success and relationships and family. Hell is being dependant on something for life that cannot deliver. It is a substitute that cannot fill the hole. The result is the craving for salt by a man who is dying of thirst. I am so susceptible to this. I think it is good for all of us to check ourselves every once in while to make sure we have not slowly substituted something for God. When Jesus promises to never leave and never forsake us He is promising that He will always be enough even throughout all eternity. That is a promise that requires no rehab.

Verse for Reflection:

Be strong and courageous. Do not be afraid or terrified because of them, for the Lord your God goes with you; he will never leave you nor forsake you.

- Deuteronomy 31:6

The House-Shaped Idol

"Suzie" made a frantic call to my office. She needed to see a pastor and she needed to see one now. When she arrived her eyes were red rimmed and swollen. She had obviously been weeping. She sat in the chair across from me clutching a wad of tissues in her hand. Through intermittent tears she told me the story. Her husband had lost his job some time ago. He had taken a while to find another one and the one he finally found did not provide nearly the same compensation. They would have to sell their house. That sentence caused the dam to break and the tears flowed. She finally blew her nose and looked at me with her puffy eyes and said, "You don't understand. This is my dream house. I love this house. Losing my house is like losing a child."

Now, I need to tell you two things. One is that my little brother died in a motorcycle accident and I watched as the grief rolled over my parents in waves. The other fact you should know is on every spiritual gift survey I have ever taken I score the lowest for the gift of compassion. By the way I find that for a lot of people that is pretty unacceptable for their minister. I guess the good news is that it doesn't bother me as much as it would if I scored higher. That seems ironic doesn't it?

Anyway, when "Suzie" said that to me I think I snorted. I was pretty surprised that anyone would compare a house to a child and I was also fairly offended. Looking back I should have been more pastoral. "Suzie" got pretty mad at my lack of compassion, left my office, and left the church. As far as I know she has not been back.

By being more pastoral I don't mean holding her hand and telling her how sorry I was she was losing something so precious. I mean I should have recognized an idol. Had I been in the jungles and some man came running up to me with a ring in his nose and a spear in his hand screaming and crying because someone had stolen his household idol I would not have snorted. I would not have held his hand and tried to comfort him in the loss of something so precious. I would have seized the opportunity to tell him about the true God. I would have told him that the idol was simply made of wood and stone and really could not fill up the emptiness in him. But the God of heaven and earth had given his Son as a sacrifice and now the emptiness in his soul could be filled. It would be a marvelous chance to share the Gospel.

If I could have another shot at "Suzie" I would have told her that. "Suzie" has not come back so I am telling you just in case you have ever sounded like "Suzie" when one of your dreams has popped like a balloon and you feel like your heart will never heal. Maybe it was more than a dream that popped. Maybe it was an idol. If it was then as precious as it was it is a gift you have been given. The hole in your chest is open again and the true God is ready to move into the place He belongs.

Verse for Reflection:

And God spoke all these words: "I am the Lord your God, who brought you out of Egypt, out of the land of slavery. You shall have no other gods before me."

- Exodus 20:1-3

The Marker is Always Called

Once a year I have the opportunity to speak at a small church in South Florida. The community is a pretty exclusive place. Yesterday I watched as private jets took off and landed on the airstrip squeezed between the clay tennis courts and the championship golf course. Word on the street is that Vice President Joe Biden will be playing golf today on one of the courses here in this gated community. I think you get the picture.

I was talking with my host yesterday about the impact of the economic downturn we have experienced the last couple of years. Downturn is a good word for it. Think of a cliff with multiple levels. If you make 30k per year you are only three levels up and the fall to the ground is just not that far. But here in this community there are people who seem closer to the clouds than the ground and the fall can be very great indeed. My host told me there had been four suicides in this little slice of paradise since the bubble burst. The fall was very great indeed.

There isn't a person here who would tell me that their house or their boat or their plane is worth their life. So, what happened? No one starts out thinking they are worshiping their work or the fruit of their labor or loins. It just slowly happens. But, make no mistake. Every god eventually calls in its marker. That seems to be what it means to be a god. When the marker is called is when you suddenly realize you have a god and it is time to give your sacrifice however great it might be. I don't know all that went into the suicides here but I do know a call went out from a god. It was clear as a bell.

Making a gift from God into a god we serve is a slow process. I am sure when the millions were rolling in, the men who would eventually take their lives never thought that with the money came a grave danger. They looked at the fruit of their labor and they rejoiced and maybe even thanked God for their good fortune. The parent who welcomes a newborn sits cradling the baby in their arms and does not know they hold a great and wonderful danger.

Every god eventually demands sacrifice. It may start small. Long hours at the office or scrimping and saving so your child can go to college. But gods demand sacrifices and eventually they demand blood. Here in this oceanfront community a god showed up and demanded life itself.

The real God has reversed the flow of this river that runs through every human heart. This God provides the sacrifice Himself. He always has. From the ram caught in the thicket that took the place of Isaac to the limp body of the Nazarene hanging lifeless on a cross. There is no God like our God.

Remember that today and rejoice. The gift of life is the gift of God Himself. Don't confuse Him with the other gifts He provides as wonderful as they may be. That mistake can be deadly.

Verse for Reflection:

"You are my witnesses," declares the Lord, "and my servant whom I have chosen, that you may know and believe me and understand that I am he. Before me no god was formed, nor shall there be any after me."

- Isaiah 43:10

LeBron Cuts to Pieces

I live in Cleveland, Ohio. There is nothing spectacular about Cleveland. You can tell when someone asks you where you are from and you say, "Cleveland." Tell someone you are from Colorado or the coast of California or even Chicago or Pittsburgh and you will get some kind of response. But Cleveland is different. It sounds like a city you see in black and white. It is simply grey.

Maybe that is why we are so desperate for a championship in some sport. Let us hold a trophy over our heads and our city will blaze with color if even for a moment. I think that is part of the reason people responded with such ferocity when LeBron left to take his talents to South Beach. LeBron was our hope for living color.

There is an interesting passage in the book of Ezekiel. It is a long parable of a young woman who runs away from the lover of her soul and plays the harlot with anyone and everyone. It is a very graphic tale told in first person by God Himself. At one point God, who in the parable is playing the role of the faithful husband, says he is going to allow the lovers to come and surround his dear wife. He says with tears streaming down his face that they will strip her naked and will cut her to pieces. When I read the chapter for the first time it struck me as strange. I understood she had hell to pay but it really seemed the punishment should have come from the husband. But the husband just removes his protection and allows his wife and her lovers to finish the play they had started. The play ends in tragedy.

A god is something you put your trust in. It is the trust that this thing or this person will give us what our soul most deeply needs and desires. All other gods eventually demand the life of the one who worships them. In the parable the woman finally begins to lose her appeal to her paramours and they turn on her and discard her like so much trash. She had forsaken the lover of her soul for them and now she stood while they cursed her and walked away laughing. So it is with every god. The mother whose daughter screams, "I hate you" and the words pierce her soul like a dagger. Her god has come to cut her to pieces. The businessman who is handed a pink slip after giving all his prime years to be a company man sits on his couch at home and weeps. His god has cut him to pieces. I watched people take off Cleveland Cavalier jerseys and put them in a pile the night of "The Decision" and light them on fire. A hometown god had cut them to pieces.

In the parable in Ezekiel the story does not end with the woman in pieces. Instead the story ends with the husband saying that he will make atonement for her. This is a husband who is willing to move heaven and earth to get her back. He is the one who is willing to bind up her wounds caused by the lovers she had cheated with. The atonement would cost him his life. Atonement always does. There is only one God who is willing to give His life for yours. And by His stripes you are healed.

Verse for Reflection:

I am the good shepherd; I know my sheep and my sheep know me— just as the Father knows me and I know the Father—and I lay down my life for the sheep.

- John 10: 14-15

Net Worth

The news this week has been all about the stock market. I read yesterday that Americans have lost several trillion dollars in net worth this past 2 weeks. The plunge has been breathtaking. I have been thinking of the term "net worth." I feel like God has been teaching me over and over the last several months that my worth needs to be placed in Him and Him alone. I tend to look for worth and value in all kinds of things. I don't feel preoccupied with my worth until I notice how much I compare myself with other people and how important what other people think is to me.

Anyway, back to the market. I was thinking of how God must look at us and the closest I can get is how I look at my teenage daughter. Becca has a domain in our house that we have given over to her. It is her room. It is where she keeps her stuff and we let her keep her stuff however she wants as long as we can close her door. At times it looks like a clothes bomb went off sometime during the night in there. We provide the most important things in her life. All the stuff in her room is stuff she has accumulated over the last nearly 18 years.

I was thinking what it would be like if something happened that reduced her stuff to less than half of what it is now. Maybe someone would come in with huge garbage bags and began to just load up a bunch of stuff indiscriminately. It would definitely cause Becca some pain. I on the other hand might look into her room and think it a good thing. Now if she wailed that her "net worth" had been reduced I would sit her down and look her in the eyes and say, "Oh, honey, all that stuff had nothing to do with your worth. Look me in the eyes and see the love I have for you. If your room is completely empty this love for you will not go away, it will not fade. You are mine, my princess, the apple of my eye and in the midst of your cleaned out room we will have a wonderful time just the two of us."

So, as I have watched my room get cleaned out these last couple of weeks I have been sitting in a cleaned out room with the Lord of the universe and listened carefully about how He really feels about me. I can sit and wail as the garbage bags are hauled out of my room or I can run to my Father, the One who owns the whole house, and sit with Him until I remember what my net worth is really based on.

Verse for Reflection:

Naked I came from my mother's womb, and naked I will depart. The Lord gave and the Lord has taken away; may the name of the Lord be praised."

- Job 1:21

Pg. 67

Summer, Fudgesicles, and Jesus

It's officially summer. I know because I have found my frozen delight of the year. This year it is the fudgesicle. Fudgesicles are 80 calories of refreshing deliciousness. I am eating them like they are going out of style. Every summer it seems like I hit on something like this. There have been popsicles, icees, homemade slurpees. You name it, if it is frozen and sweet I have binged on it during the summer.

I read somewhere recently that real appetites are different than artificial appetites. An appetite for something real doesn't seem like it is seasonal. I don't only thirst for water in the Spring (no pun intended). There is also something about a real appetite that allows for a feeling of contentment. I eat a fudgesicle and I begin walking over to the freezer before I have sucked the stick clean. Then after two more fudgesicles I am ready for something salty. It is a circus over here. Now you know why I exercise so much.

Anyway, fudgesicles got me thinking about Jesus. My appetite for God is not seasonal and for that I am very thankful. After time with Jesus there is an experience of contentment. I don't bounce from sweet to salty. My appetite for the eternal runs deep within me and is satisfied only by a relationship with God Himself.

The amazing thing is that God has made Himself available to me every day and every hour. My stash of fudgesicles is running low even as I write. But tomorrow morning God will be waiting for me in my quiet room and will give me as much of Himself as I can stand. So, I will fill up and walk out of that room content and knowing that the deepest hunger inside of me has been filled by that which is real. Fudgesicles are good but I was created for something a little more solid and so were you.

This summer go ahead and treat yourself to some frozen delights but don't go a day without delighting yourself in the One who made you and offers to fill you up to the brim with what your soul really longs for... Himself.

Verse for Reflection:

You, God, are my God, earnestly I seek you; I thirst for you, my whole being longs for you, in a dry and parched land where there is no water.

- Psalm 63:1

Pg. 68

Jesus and My Father-in-Law

Early yesterday morning my father-in-law had a stroke. He was getting out of bed and discovered that his right side was paralyzed. We have spent the last 2 days running back and forth to the hospital and trying to figure out what it all means. He has recovered much of his feeling in his right side but they are keeping him in the hospital for a while.

My father-in-law is one of my favorite people. It is not just that he raised my wife to be the wonderful person she is but 35 years ago he gave his life to Jesus and has become a really amazing person. I sat with him in ICU just the two of us. I asked him how he felt about having a stroke. It was one of those questions you don't often have the chance to ask. I was asking how he felt about growing old. I was asking not just how he felt about the possibility of dying but of dying like this with tiny explosions in his brain that would take life away little by little.

It tells you something about my father-in-law that I felt free to ask him such a thing in the middle of ICU. He laughed his normal little laugh and then looked at me and said, "Well, you know me Joe. I like to be active. I really like to be active. But if God has other plans then He has other plans." And then he said, "I know what my first priority is. I want to impact these people." And he pointed to the nurses and aids walking around outside the room.

My father-in-law admittedly didn't know God's long term plans for him but he could see His short term plans. He was saying that he didn't know about recovery or future strokes but he did know that right now he was in ICU and as far as he could tell it was as good a mission field as any. My father in law has a way with people. Everyone who has ever spent any time with him at all falls in love with him. It is a great trait to have.

I think I saw at least some of the reason why. He never looks past them to the next thing. The people in his path are not obstacles to get by in order to get where he is going. They are their own destination and for them it feels absolutely wonderful. I have to believe that is the way people felt around Jesus. After 35 years of walking with Jesus my father-in-law is acting just like Him. And right now the two of them are in ICU on a short term mission trip and the people in Akron City Hospital may never be the same.

Verse for Reflection:

He said to them, "Go into all the world and preach the gospel to all creation."

- Mark 16:15

Treasures You Know Not

Brittany plays soccer on my daughter's team. When my kids play sports I am vaguely aware of other people being in the stands. My wife is much more in tune with people than with the actual game although she watches the game. I on the other hand like to sit or stand by myself and watch. I don't multi-task especially at sporting events.

Anyway, I could probably have picked Brittany's parents out of a line up but I had never talked to them really. I would do the polite nod and smile and then my face would return to the slightly concerned look of the too competitive father. Yesterday I was visiting my father-in-law in the hospital (he is doing much better and came home from the hospital today). We were talking when his doctor came in to check on him. It was Brittany's dad. He was very friendly and professional and obviously knew what he was doing. By the time he left I was feeling grateful my father-in-law was in such good hands.

That night I went to the soccer game. I looked forward to seeing Brittany's dad just to say hello. I found it fascinating how quickly my feelings had changed toward him. I looked up at the stands and scanned the faces of the parents watching their daughters play. I wondered what each one did for a living or how each of our lives might touch each other away from the soccer field.

I blunder through so much of life unaware of the gifts that crowd around me. I remember C.S.Lewis writing that a person, any person, is the most magnificent thing you will ever encounter outside of God Himself. Yesterday I found myself really seeing Dr. Chung for the first time. I was thankful for how God had gifted him and thought this treasure has been sitting next to me all year and I never even noticed.

I guess I am inviting you to look around today. The person behind you at Starbucks may be the one who one day saves your life or you theirs. The world is full of jewels and they all have names even if you don't know them yet.

Verse for Reflection:

A new commandment I give to you, that you love one another: just as I have loved you, you also are to love one another. By this all people will know that you are my disciples, if you have love for one another.

- John 13:34-35

Living Water

A couple of weeks ago, I went on an epic bicycle ride with a team from our church. On one of the days we rode a little over 100 miles. That's a pretty long way to peddle. At one point we stopped by a sign displaying the temperature at 95 degrees and had our picture taken. We wanted it on record. At the very end of the ride I was out of water. I held each water bottle to my mouth and squeezed the last drops out and then kept riding. The last few miles all I could think of was water.

The other night our Bible study was looking at the fourth chapter of John. Jesus is sitting at a well when a woman comes to draw water. I have a scene in my head. The place is dusty and arid. Jesus sits with his back against the stone of the well with His feet jutting out in front of Him. The woman comes to draw water and Jesus puts his hand up to shade His eyes from the noonday sun. They talk about water. Actually they begin by talking about thirst.

The Gospel is always in that order. Thirst comes first and then the water. But when the water comes it is not just enough to get a couple of gulps or even a couple of buckets. It is a flood. A geyser. It is enough to jump in and splash around in. It is water to waste—in a land that has never been able to waste water.

When I pulled in from the 100-mile bike ride I wanted more than just a fresh water bottle. I wanted a pool of water and that is exactly where I headed. With bottled water in both fists I flipped off my biking shoes and headed to the hotel pool. It was exquisite.

I love the way the prophet Isaiah puts it in his 55th chapter:

"Ho, everyone who thirsts, come to the waters. Come buy wine and milk without money and without cost. Why do you spend your money on what does not satisfy and your wages on what is not food. Listen carefully to me and eat what is good and delight yourself in abundance of fare."

When I go to God it is more than just a gulp of water I need. I want the whole pool. I want what Jesus promised which is a spring, a geyser flowing up to eternal life. Don't settle for less.

Verse for Reflection:

Jesus answered and said to her, "Everyone who drinks of this water shall thirst again; but whoever drinks of the water that I shall give him shall never thirst; but the water that I shall give him shall become in him a well of water springing up to eternal life."

- John 4:13-14

PART V
You've Been Gifted

You've Been Gifted

What would happen if a group of people decided to try to bring back the Spirit of Christmas with 10,000 spontaneous acts of generosity in the month of December? I really had no idea when I had 10,000 "You've Been Gifted" cards ordered. The cards are pretty simple and just explain that at Christ

Community Chapel we believe the greatest gift ever given was Jesus and the gift we are giving now is just a reminder of the generosity of God. The idea was for everyone in church to take a couple of cards and move out into the community looking for people to give something to.

Remember:

For God so loved the world that He gave His one and only Son, that whosoever believes in Him shall not perish but have everlasting life.

- John 3:16

It has been a blast to hear the stories that come back. The stories range from buying a cup of coffee to banking cord blood, from making home-made gifts to tackling a mugger. God works in all ways. Here are some of the stories from both the gifters and giftees...

Story 1: One of God's angels gifted me. She didn't know how much it meant and was needed. Please send a thank you to your congregation and to the "angel" at Walmart.

Story 2: I 'gifted' a frail, sweet, old woman at the grocery store recently. What pleasure was on her face afterwards. I think that it took her the several minutes walking to her car to digest what had happened. She walked back in to bring her cart back and thanked me more and gave me the most precious hug ever. This is so much fun! It is so rewarding and the best Christmas gift for me too. I feel guilty for the joy that this brings me. I know I am getting far more doing this than anyone is getting from the free gifts. It is almost addicting.

Story 3: I have traditionally had a difficult time around the holidays due to what we as a culture have done with this most sacred celebration. I have not felt such joy in a long time. I have had so much fun doing spontaneous and sometimes anonymous gifting acts. I have felt like old Ebenezer on Christmas day–this has been one of my best Christmases ever!

Story 4: God really used the "You've Been Gifted" campaign to impact my family. My parents were stunned when I asked the server for the check of the young couple across from us in a restaurant. For my parents, church is more of a social place where they have great friendships. I have talked with them for years about having a relationship with Christ and being born-again, and those "You've Been Gifted" cards opened up a door to share God's truth with them again. I had to hold back the tears in the restaurant when I realized once again that God's ways are not our ways, and that He calls us to obedience.

Story 5: A young man who attends our church is a server in a restaurant. A co-worker of his who happens to be Muslim asked him if he attended Christ Community Chapel. He said yes. She then told him that someone had picked up the check for another table and handed her the card to present since they wanted to be anonymous. She said she had never seen anything like that and thought it was awesome.

Story 6: I wanted to share my experience using the "You've Been Gifted" card. I was in the Super Walmart recently and asked the Lord before entering the store to

lead me to someone who needs a blessing. I really felt the presence of God while choosing a check-out aisle. I ended up behind a woman in a wheelchair-cart, and she was with her adult daughter. They were having trouble paying for their purchases and were trying to use different credit cards. It was obvious that this was the person God has chosen me to 'gift.'

I stepped next to the lady and said, "Merry Christmas! Why don't you let me pay for you today." The cashier overheard me and said, "You can't do that." I asked, "Why not?" She turned the cash register's monitor toward me that showed her total bill was $192. I said, "That's okay. Our church asked us to look for opportunities to bless others this Christmas season." I then handed her the "You've Been Gifted" card. The lady in the wheelchair began crying really hard, and her eyes were red. She grabbed my face in her hands and said, "Thank you very much. I didn't think kindness like this still existed." She then said the reason she was shopping today is to buy clothes for her husband's funeral that weekend.

The cashier heard this and raised her hands in the air (and held them there) saying, "Praise God!" She then asked where our church was, and said she would like to go to a church where people are as nice as me. At this point, I was feeling awkward about all the attention and started to babble phrases like, "It's not a big deal," and "I have a lot of money" – how embarrassing is that!

However, after all was said and done, it really felt great to "team up" with God be a part of blessing someone else.

Story 7: I am excited to share this "You've Been Gifted" experience because I am so thankful that when we ask, God truly answers our prayers. The problems arise when we (I) aren't patient and refuse to listen to Him. Instead, we (I) try to make up our own answers–which often best suits what we (I) think is best.

That said, here's my story!

This year and the past few years have been very financially challenging and stressful. This year I felt God leading me to try giving 4 "You've Been Gifted" cards away, one for each week before Christmas. Well, somehow, I ended up with 6 cards.

So I began to pray for guidance for the best way to give these cards away and the amount I should spend on the gifts. There was a lot that was unknown to me. How was I going to get the money to spend on the gifts? Who would be the right people to receive the gifts? I wanted the gifts to make a difference and have an impact.

Last year, I just bought Starbucks coffee for someone, handed them a "You've Been Gifted" card, spoke a few words to them, and was done—easy enough. This year, I felt there needed to be more effort on my part.

While listening to one of the "gifted" stories shared at church, I knew the place to give these gifts away—the Goodwill store. So all I had to do was figure out the amounts to spend.

I received an e-mail from church requesting a volunteer to help in the nursery on a Sunday, after I had just served on that Saturday. I had so much to do to start getting ready for Christmas, so I was hesitant to volunteer again. When the 8:45 a.m. Sunday service was over, I was just going to skip out on volunteering and head home to my busy, busy day. I walked out of the sanctuary and felt like I got shoved towards the children's check-in area. There I found the Childcare Director, and as usual, she was scurrying around making sure all was good. Since I saw her, I offered to help. She said all was covered, but thanked me for being willing to serve. Then she reached into her pocket, pulled out something, handed it to me, and said, "This is just a small thank you for always being so willing to help. Merry Christmas!"

Lo and behold, it was a $10 gift card to Walmart. I thought, "Thank You God. This must be my amount." I do catering, and had recently done an early Christmas party earning an extra tip of $50. So, I had 6 cards to give, and $60 (in cash and a gift card). Do the math. I don't think God needed to be more specific.

This may seem a bit more detailed than needed, or it may even seem crazy! I just wanted to share because I am so thankful that if I trust God, He will answer and provide! God, through our church, has let me grow tremendously. I have attended church all my life, but Christ Community Chapel is a place where God is at work, and I am very thankful for the opportunity to be a part of the "big" picture here. Thanks for allowing me to share this little story.

Story 8: We went to Flemings restaurant tonight just to try to not think about our little girl who passed away. While there, we talked to the owner who goes to our church, and he told us he would pray for us at the deacons' meeting tomorrow. While sitting at dinner, we saw a guy eating alone. I got a feeling to use a "You've Been Gifted" card even though Christmas was over. We told the waitress that we wanted to buy his meal for him compliments of Hudson Chapel (I struggle with remembering the new name of our church, Christ Community Chapel). As he left, he came over to our table and told us that he was a pastor in southern Ohio, and this gift made his night. He said he was going to tell his church about it. In the midst of such sorrow, we began to laugh and smile knowing Christ was working. This was one of the hardest days of our lives, and the Lord just said to us, "I am in control." This was so awesome. As we were going to pay for the checks, our waitress told us that the owner had picked up our check! He had planned on doing this before he found out we gave a "You've Been Gifted" card/gift to this other man. This story shows that God is so good.

Story 9: My "gifted" story is slightly different. I knew a single, young lady who was struggling and unemployed, and I knew she didn't have a Christmas tree.

So I stopped at her house yesterday and told her "You've been gifted!" Then I gave her a homemade Christmas tree.

The joy on someone's face after being gifted is priceless. As was this young lady when I handed her a Christmas tree. I started to cry when she was stunned.

Most responses are why would someone do this? Hopefully they will look for answers by going to church.

Story 10: I have a very interesting story that is only possible through God and from God. Nine months ago my husband left me and my one-year-old daughter to be with a 21 year old. I was pregnant at the time and now have a newborn son. We have recently decided to try to reconcile and restore our marriage. However, his mistress is pregnant.

My mother and I have learned so much about God's love through Christ Community Chapel. I cannot tell you how much healing and hope God has brought us through this church. I've really tried to focus my heart on the fruits of the spirit and let them shine even in the darkest hour of my life thus far. I've even been kind and understanding to my husband's mistress from the beginning–that is not me, it's the Lord for sure! She's been emotionally unstable from the start but even more so with my husband coming back to us.

Recently, I had a long conversation with her, and she was awed by how I could be so nice to her–again, not me, all God! She e-mailed my mom the next morning, and after a few e-mails back and forth, my mom offered to buy her the baby furniture she needs for her new baby! My mom has been right there with me through every tear and forced smile, so for her to offer to do this is amazing! We are not by any means rich, but my mom saw that this girl needs help and gave it. She even offered to baby-sit once the baby comes. This girl has a very small support system and needs help and to see how kindness and forgiveness is for everyone, not just our friends and family. I know that if my husband and I are able to restore our marriage, her baby (and maybe even her) will be a loved member of our family. I said I was going to try and shorten the story, but it is just full of God's blessings and what He can do with people's hearts. I think we've all been "gifted" in this situation! I thank God for this wonderful church.

Story 11: Jim Colledge, the founding pastor of Christ Community Chapel, was at the deli counter at a local grocery store. There were dozens of meat and cheese packages up on the counter, and he thought they were pre-made so reached up for one. The deli worker said, "No, those aren't for you. They are for pick-up. Someone ordered all of these." Jim thought, "That's nuts!" Just then a young couple from Christ Community Chapel walked up. They told him they were inspired by the "You've Been Gifted" campaign and decided to make lunches for every delivery driver in their company. 150 drivers received lunch the next day with a card that read "You've Been Gifted."

Story 12: A guy from Christ Community Chapel was at a local mall, couldn't find a parking space, and decided to wait in the parking lot to grab a space. A woman was walking out of the mall when a guy comes up, shoves her, grabs all her shopping bags, and takes off running. Our guy jumps out of his truck, sets a course to intersect, and nails this guy, knocking him off his feet into a snow bank. The robber dropped the bags, got up, and ran away. So our guy picks up the bags, knocks the snow off the stuff, and walks back to the woman. She was beside herself, grateful, and wanted to pay the guy or do something for him. So, he comes to his senses (think adrenaline rush) and says something along the lines of, "No, but I have something for you." He reaches into his pocket and hands her a "You've Been Gifted" card.

Story 13: I would like to share my version of a "You've Been Gifted" story that has a twist.

I have sat in church and listened to Pastor Joe share e-mails and letters of the "gifted" stories. I have been brought to tears and felt warmth in my heart as I've listened to them. I am in awe of what the members of our church have done to make people's lives brighter. I love the idea of the cards, but I must admit, I take them, but I have never used any.

This Christmas season, I was determined to use a card! I looked around but never felt led to buy coffee or pay for anyone's groceries. I started to wonder what was wrong with me–then it hit me–I had been "gifted," and I wanted to share that story. I teach fifth and sixth grade. I "loop" with my kids, meaning I keep them for two years. I have a new group of fifth graders this year, and I think I am in love–they are the sweetest group of kids I have had in 21 years. I promise I am getting to my story...

I have a very dear teacher friend who lives in Iowa. Her husband has been battling leukemia for 3 years and last April finally received a stem cell transplant to save his life. He had a very difficult road, and is still on it today. He has lost over 60 pounds and is fighting stomach issues daily. Then, in June, my friend's mom was diagnosed with early stage colon cancer. After surgery, she seems to be okay. Then, her worst nightmare happened in August–my friend's 11 year old son was diagnosed with sinus cancer. He is currently in the middle of 43 weeks of chemo and 6 weeks of radiation. I have felt so helpless. I have sent almost daily e-mails, weekly calls, and sent gift cards. It sure didn't seem like enough. So, in my quest to make little servants out of my students, I began to share my friend's story with my kids. We talked about her rough journey. However, I felt like they needed to hear about a young man their age and what he was going through. During our "quote of the day" time, we always talked about this young man and how he was doing. I decided that they could impact his life in a big way. We took pictures of our class, we talked about him, and the kids set out to write him personal letters at Thanksgiving time. Their letters brought tears to my eyes. They were so heartfelt and honest. We then sent them off and waited for a response. My friend called and through her tears said that her son had read every one, and that our photos were hanging in his room at home. The kids were thrilled.

Next up were letters to our troops in Afghanistan. A co-worker has a cousin serving, so off went wonderful letters thanking them for their service. Again, they were sweet, heartfelt, and moving. They took such care in creating them. Last to end the holiday season, we made no-sew blankets for the "Linus Project" at Akron Children's Hospital for babies in the NICU. These kids loved this project, and they wanted to know about the babies they were going to help give warmth to. It was pure joy.

Lastly, on a personal front, I always donate to a charity

at Christmas. This year, my donation was a "Flat Daddy" to a military family who has a parent deployed. They are cardboard cut-outs with the parent's photo so the kids can feel their parent's presence at home.

Finally, the end.... My story is not how I spent money doing good for others, but rather it is how my heart was "gifted" by the kind, generous, and heartfelt deeds I saw others doing for people in need. My heart grew about 10 sizes this Christmas, and I only spent money on postage! So, I am thankful that the church always shares the stories of being "gifted." I love those, and they remind me to think of others rather than myself. I just wanted to share a story of how I was "gifted" without a card.

Story 14: This morning while returning from driving kids to school (yes, I was still in my PJs and slippers), I came across a broken-down car with two young men looking lost as to what to do. The funniest thing about this is that I always take the second road into our development. For some reason this morning, I took the first road, which is where I found the car in the middle of the road.

I asked if they needed help. One young man replied that his friend was going to take him to the bank to get money to pay the tow truck, which means the car would have remained in the middle of the road. I asked him what was wrong with it, and he said he had just bought the car for $1,100 from Craig's List, and the transmission fluid spewed out everywhere.

So, I called my mechanic (a Christian), and asked him to have the car towed to his shop at my expense. The young man was so ecstatic, he hugged me and said, "thank you" a million times. I responded with, "Merry Christmas. Just remember what it's all about and get your butt to church." He said he attends a local church.

The coolest parts of this story are that (1) I took a road that I never take in order for God to lead me to these guys, and (2) the towing company called me later to say they had ripped up my debit card slip because our friend, the mechanic, wanted to take care of the bill himself.

I am blessed beyond measure. I am thankful for getting the encouragement needed from our church to do these things. It's awesome!

Story 15: When the "You've Been Gifted" cards came out this year, I grabbed a couple and put them in my wallet. I love the idea of showing the love of Christ through random acts of kindness, but it took me some time to actually use one

Pg. 81

of them. This probably sounds really dumb, but I'm kind of timid with strangers, and the idea of going up to somebody and paying for their stuff just made me really nervous. I had a little fear that they would freak out and not let me pay for anything. I can't tell you how many times I pulled the little card out of my wallet, ready to pay for the person behind me, and ended up stuffing it back in because I got too nervous. But, recently I was out to lunch with my friend, and opened my wallet to get my debit card, and the gifted card came out with it. I turned around and told the people behind me, a woman and her college-aged daughter, that I would love to buy their food for them then explained the meaning behind it. They both were so thankful, and the woman gave me a huge hug. I was so touched by their response that I almost started crying right there, wondering how I could have ever held back from doing this before. The woman told me that I had made her day, but really she had made mine. It was such an awesome reminder to see the true joy that comes with giving for the Lord.

Story 16: My 8 year old daughter has dance class in the city of Akron. We always travel Route 8 and get off on the Tallmadge Avenue exit. Each week there is a man at the exit who is homeless. After I reminded my daughter of dance today, a few minutes later she came in my office with a bag of items. In the bag was food, a card she made stating, "Merry Christmas, I love God," a stuffed animal, and some of her money. She included a "You've Been Gifted" card. This was all for the homeless man. I truly felt seeing her thoughtfulness and generosity was a gift to me too. I am so glad we do this campaign each year.

Story 17: This is a unique story of generosity. My 3 year old grand daughter was at the doctor this past Wednesday for a minor issue when they realized that she had some symptoms that could indicate a really serious illness. It's amazing how quickly things get into perspective when something like this happens. Suddenly, this busy week of Christmas shopping and baking has turned into a week of fervent prayer with doctor visits and blood tests. It included a lot of tears and of course some sleepless nights as well. My daughter (who is the little girl's mom) was scheduled to be induced to deliver her third baby girl at that point too. So you can imagine what an emotional week it has been for her and for all of us. Now, here's the awesome part. In hearing about all of this, a young family from our church called and said they wanted to pay for the "cord blood" from the new baby to be saved and banked in case her sister needs it. This process costs $2,000-$3,000, and I can't think of a more touching act of generosity. It motivated me to want to do the same. I love our church!

Story 18: This is a very cool "You've Been Gifted" story. First, I wanted to suggest that everyone at our church remembers to keep the "gifted" cards on hand. When I had the opportunity to "gift" someone, I didn't have a card with me, but that didn't stop me from jumping on the opportunity.

I haven't been feeling much in the Christmas spirit this year. I'm a little down in the dumps and just all over "blah" this year. Regardless, I was at the bank the other day when a deaf man came in with his cab driver. The deaf man was trying to cash a check to pay the cab driver, but his account was overdrawn by $67. He couldn't pay the $21 cab fare because his account was negative. I told the teller I wanted to take care of the negative balance, but before she could do so, a lady at the other end of the counter took the opportunity and said, "Merry Christmas" to the deaf man and his cab driver. I felt robbed! (Haha!) Robbed of my opportunity to share the many blessings the Lord has bestowed upon me and my family. I have three healthy kids, a husband who protects, provides, and loves me, and an extended family that I have grown close to over the years. To top it all off, I still have both of my parents who are 72 and 73 and have been married for 52 years. God has been so good to me, and I remain so undeserving.

So, I asked the teller to withdraw money from my personal account, and I handed a stack of $20 bills to the deaf man, telling him, "Merry Christmas." He signed, "Thank you," and I could see how grateful he was. I only wish I'd had a "You've Been Gifted" card to give him so he could have come to our church to learn of the greatest gift of all.

I am thankful for such a wonderful campaign. I can't help but wonder if the other woman at the bank was also from our church. I kind of hope not because it would be awesome to know there are many others out there spreading the blessings of Christmas.

Story 19: It was Christmas Eve, and I walked into a local grocery store to do some last minute shopping. As I stood at the check-out, a woman was standing in front of me. I felt this sense of urgency to gift her, but I wasn't prepared–I did have a "gifted" card in my pocket, and I didn't have enough cash and would have to use a credit card. She had a ham and all the rest of the fixings for a Christmas dinner. There was a lot of food there, and I thought, oh dear, I probably shouldn't be spending this much (my husband had just regained employment after being laid off, and things were tight). On the other hand, I was grateful for God's provision for our family through that difficult time, and I hadn't talked to my husband about spending that much at once. For a second, I waffled, then that sense of urgency came over me again to just do it! So I did. I "gifted" her.

She turned to me in shock with tears in her eyes and asked me how I knew she needed the help. I said I didn't, but that God knew her circumstances, and that He cared about her (not at all what I had prepared to say). She then explained how she had been in the hospital, was just released, and stopped on her way home to pick up food. She said it had been very difficult financially for her, and she was about to spend all that she had on the food. It was as if time stood still as I, the woman, the clerk, and the bagger stood by and watched as God worked. We were all blown away! I could hardly drive home because I cried the whole way!

I am not an eloquent writer, and so I fear that I am in the way of God's message. This story is just one example of many. I am so thankful that God has placed me under Pastor Joe's leading and teaching–he is a great pastor. I have been challenged to go beyond myself in all areas of my Christian walk. Our church teaches us how to be obedient to God in our journey.

I look forward to what is ahead, especially as I go out armed with scripture and a "You've Been Gifted" card. This time, rather than trying to "work it," I'm just going to be ready to participate in God's work.

Story 20: My story is short, but I was struck this morning at Starbucks when I decided to pay for the coffee of the person behind me in line. After quietly whispering to the barista of my desire, she immediately whispered back to me "Okay, do you have your 'You've Been Gifted' card with you?" What does that say about the people of our town and more importantly the impact of our church right here at home? That experience served to encourage me to want to reach further and impact one more person and then one more after that.

I'm think the campaign should be reworded to say "You and I Have Been Gifted!"

Story 21: I was standing in line at our local grocery store, but then I realized I forgot something, so I left the line. When I got back to a new line, a girl was in front of me, and God spoke to me and said, "Pay for her tab." I didn't have any

Pg. 84

"You've Been Gifted" cards, so as she was finishing I looked at her and said I would pay, but the gift was from Christ Community Chapel, and I didn't have any little cards to give her. She looked at me completely astounded and said, "Wow, my family just visited there for the first time today!" I said, "Well this is a sign that you are not supposed to be a stranger." She said, "I guess so!" She then told me how she knows she is supposed to come back to our church. Pretty cool, huh?

Thank God that I forgot something and had to get out of line.

I am just disappointed that I didn't chase her down and ask if she knew the Lord–but I was stuck in line at that point.

Story 22: When the "You've Been Gifted" campaign started at Christmas, I took three cards. The first card was easy. I gave it to my hairdresser along with prepayment for a haircut. I told her to pick one of her clients and give her a free haircut. She was thrilled and said she knew exactly who to give it to, a recently widowed woman who was coming in that week and had been stretching her appointments because money was tight.

The second one was a few days before Christmas in a grocery store and required a bit more courage on my part. A young mom with a little boy was ahead of me in line. There was an issue with the person ahead of her who was using food stamps and coupons and a bad check to pay for a huge grocery cart of food. God said to me, "Use the card." I said back, "Surely not! Those people are trying to pull one over on the cashier, and their bill is over $200! Open your eyes, God. I can't be part of that!" His responded, "Open your eyes! Look right in front of you." The young mom ahead of me had a small order of very practical stuff including eggs, milk, and bread. She was being exceedingly patient and kind with the mess in front of her. I accepted God's challenge, and I waited while the cashier finished with the women in front then moved on to the young mom. My heart was pounding so loudly, I was sure everyone could hear it! Why was this so hard? As she told her the total, I brushed past her, debit card in hand and told her I wanted to buy her groceries. She looked at me with disbelief and said, "Do you mean it? Is this real?" I gave her the card and a brief explanation then paid her bill. When I looked up, the cashier was crying. She said, "Well, doesn't that beat all. I've never seen anything like it." The young mom thanked me over and over. I left thanking God all the way home for His perfect timing and gentle nudge.

I had one card left, and Christmas came and went. I kept the card with the cell phone so I saw it every day. I hadn't felt that special push from God to use it, but I was confident He would. The campaign was over, but why? Did it need to be? I looked at the card. There was no mention of Christmas. Couldn't people stand to be gifted any time of year? I waited.

January was coming to a close.

Finally, God gave me the signal! It was a blustery, cold day. I had been running errands and had noticed how filthy my car had gotten. I knew my husband would want it clean for church the next day, and I rarely ran it through the car wash. To please him, I decided to stop and get it cleaned. There was a line, and I was aware that there were some really cold young men working while I sat comfortably in my warm car. I had exact change for the car wash and paid, moving forward when the line moved. God nudged me saying, "Use the card. Those boys can use the money." I smiled. Cool! I was going to give a "big" tip and wrap it around the card. Going through the machine, I opened my wallet thinking a nice $5 bill would be great. But, I didn't have a $5 bill. I had just used it and a few singles for the car wash. All I had was a $20! My first thought was I can't do it. I'm supposed to be cutting back, tightening up the budget, cutting expenses. Times are tough, but God said, "So? That's My point. They need the money and the encouragement." I grabbed the $20, wrapped it around the "You've Been Gifted" card, and moved forward to have the car dried. When one of the young men opened the door and greeted me, I handed it to him and said, "Have a great day!" He said, "Gee, thanks!" I shut the door and I drove off. I looked back in the rear view mirror and saw the boys huddled together, staring in disbelief at the outrageous tip. I smiled, pulled out onto road, and thanked God once again for being so patient with me and for gifting me with such a great opportunity!

Story 23: About a week ago, I was shopping at a local grocery store, and as the cashier was ringing up my items. I started to think about the "gifted" card I had in my purse and the cash in my hand. I struggled with doing what was in my heart, because my mind was thinking something else. I didn't have the money to spend on what I was already buying, but I felt the need to help the woman next to me. As the cashier handed me my change, I grabbed the "gifted" card and put $10.00 with it on the counter next to the lady and said, "Merry Christmas." I didn't stay to talk, or explain why I did it. I guess I thought if I started to talk I would get all choked up and not be able to do it.

Our family has been struggling financially for over a year because I lost my job, due to health issues. I have been going through periods of doubt with my faith, doubt in myself, guilt, anger, etc. I tell myself to trust in God, and He will make it work. However, it has been difficult letting go.

God has a way of letting us know He's still in charge and doing miracles!

My son had a great Christmas, because I got to make him cry. I know, that doesn't sound too motherly. I told him in advance that I wasn't sure how Christmas was going to go for us this year, because we just didn't have the money to spend on gifts. He didn't ask for anything, and he was so sweet about trying to make me feel better about it.

A little boy my son knows came over recently for a play date. His mother asked me to come outside after she dropped him off. She gave me a keyboard and a Star Wars Lego kit. She told me to give them to my son and not tell him where they came from. Awesome! I hugged her and I cried. I just couldn't believe it. So, when my son opened the keyboard he cried. He told me that I shouldn't have spent the money, because we didn't have any and how did I get it. I told him that the price was right. I couldn't have asked for a better Christmas.

I don't know if the woman in the grocery store paid it forward, but I know God sure did.

Story 24: Another story is of a young guy who was driving to pick up a prescription for his father-in-law who was living with them. It was for almost $50.00 which was a lot for him. In fact he had borrowed the money from a friend and was going to pay back the friend at payday. It was a really cold winter day, and he saw a guy walking on the side of the road. He picked him up and said, "You can thank my parent's church. They have this 'You've Been Gifted' thing going. This is my gift to you." The guy said, "Christ Community Chapel, right? Yeah, I was buying gloves at a store, and some guy reached in front of me and bought me gloves and gave me a card. Pretty cool." When they reached the pharmacy, they went through the drive-through. The hitchhiker reached over the driver and paid the $50.00 then said to him, "You've been gifted!" They both laughed. The driver took this guy to his destination then went and gave his buddy the money he had borrowed and told him the story.

Two weeks later, Pastor Joe told the story to the church congregation as the "You've Been Gifted" story of the week. At the end of the service, a few people were waiting for Pastor Joe. The driver's parents were laughing because they recognized the story since their son had told them. Another guy was standing waiting to talk to Him too. He stepped up and said, "I am the hitchhiker!" Then he pointed behind him and said, "This is the guy who bought me the gloves." Amazing!

Spontaneous Generosity

When I introduced the "You've Been Gifted" cards, I think I just wanted us all to get in the giving spirit. I thought it would bring some joy to those who were the recipients of spontaneous generosity. Leave it to God to soften the hearts of long time family members, make someone feel guilty for the joy she gets in giving, and create a curiosity in the heart of a Muslim about a God who would give His Son.

God is always surprising me. It is a great game God and I play. Whenever I think I have a good idea, He takes it and changes it just enough so I realize whose idea it was in the first place. Don't miss out on what God is doing this season and every season.

Other Books by Joe Coffey

Red Like Blood

Coauthors, Joe Coffey and Bob Bevington have found that the grace of God is much more than sweet. It is also explosive, pervasive, powerful, relentless, amazing, devastating, raw, and beautiful.

Grace is deadly serious stuff. Many of our encounters with grace—the real, true grace by which God changes us one step at a time—are much more like confrontations.

These confrontations are jarring. They shake us up. Cracks appear in our carefully constructed facades. That's when grace can penetrate, Red Like Blood, flowing into those cracks, working its way deep down inside, and doing a work we could never imagine or accomplish on our own.

Smooth Stones

Street-level apologetics for everyday Christians. Because faith in Jesus makes sense, and you don't need an advanced degree to understand why. This book was written for two reasons. First, too many people think believing in Christianity means blind faith, against all evidence, the way a child believes in Santa Claus or the Tooth Fairy. Nothing could be further from the truth. Second, every few years a new book intended to undermine Christianity becomes a best seller and shakes the faith of many. Yet the arguments in these books are rarely compelling. Jesus likened faith in God to a house built on a foundation. If built on sand, storms of doubt will tear the house apart. But if we build on a solid foundation, we will stand.

In these pages, Joe Coffey inspects our foundation — so we can know why we believe, and so we can speak of our faith to others with greater confidence and clarity.